The Best Tips from
WOMEN ABOARD®

The Best Tips from
WOMEN ABOARD®

Edited by Maria Russell

Drawings by Susan Garriques

Published by
WOMEN ABOARD®
North Palm Beach, Florida

Published by *WOMEN ABOARD*®
Printed in the United States of America.

Copyright © 2000 by *WOMEN ABOARD*®

Second Printing 2002

Cover design by David Russell.

ISBN 0-9663520-1-7

Questions regarding the ordering of this book should be addressed to:
Seaworthy Publications, Inc.
215 S. Park St., Suite #1
Port Washington, WI 53074
U.S.A.
Phone: 262-268-9250
Fax: 262-268-9208
e-mail: publisher@seaworthy.com
www.seaworthy.com

To join *WOMEN ABOARD*® or for more information on THE Network for Women in Boating, call 1-877 WMN-ABRD or log on to our website at www.womenaboard.com.

WOMEN ABOARD®
is an organization dedicated to empowering women boaters.

Our goal is to enhance the boating experience
for all women in boating through
information, education, camaraderie, and support.

What began with a handful of women in 1994 has evolved into an international networking group of thousands of Sea Sisters representing nearly twenty countries.

Our monthly newsletter is the cornerstone of our network. It provides a supportive forum enabling members to ask questions and seek advice. It contains personal accounts of experiences and adventures. And it offers tips on topics such as boat maintenance, maximizing storage, updating an older boat, guests, kids, and pets.

This book is the result of a collective effort by the Sea Sisters of *WOMEN ABOARD*® who have decades of boating experience and thousands of nautical miles under their keels. We are grateful to them for sharing what they've learned.

Contributors to
The Best Tips of *WOMEN ABOARD*®

Jeanette Aden Skillings, *Brisa*, San Francisco, CA
Marcia Alley, *Gypsy*, San Antonio, TX
Donna Bakale Sherwin, *Four Seasons*, Sunnyvale, CA
Janet Bean, *Windfall*, Hilton Head, SC
Carolyn Belanger, *Sei-Max*, St. Petersburg, FL
Michael Berkenbilt, DVM, North Palm Beach, FL
Trish Birdsell-Smith, *Niki*, Nanaimo, BC
Sharon Bodkin, *Kaloki*, Norland, WA
Pat Brous, *Chilkat*
Sally Bee Brown, *Figment*, Bend, OR
Pat Campbell, *Veleiro II*, Cotuit, MA
Cheryl Carr, *Patience*, Pleasant Valley, NY
Ann Caywood, *Mañana*, Seabrook, TX
Mary Ann Chapman, *Lazarus Long*, Seattle, WA
Sue Clements, *Dos Amigos*, Houston, TX
Shirley Cooper, *Seven C's*, Holland, MI

i

Carolyn Corbett, *Bifrost*, Backus, MN
Marilyn Dawson, *Hazy Moon*, Portland, TX
Bianca DeNapoli, *Sea Reed*
Barbara DePree, *Halcyon*, Schenectady, NY
Karen Dodd, *Wings*, New Bern, NC
Chance Earle, *Countess*, Bellingham, WA
Claudia Ellis, *Kelly Anne*, Green Cove Springs, FL
Beatrice Filkins, *Joy Bells*, Islamorada, FL
Judy Fletcher, *Meander*, Nashua, NH
Faith Gerondale, *Peter Pan*, Marathon, FL
Peggy Glass, *Summer Wine*
Maggie Grantham, *Pico Blanco*, Albuquerque, MN
Colleen Gray, *Windsong*, Islamorada, FL
Mary Heckrotte, *Camryka*, Hialeah, FL
Cher Hill, *Illahee*, Sun City, FL
Linda Hill, *Nakia*, Alameda, CA
Barb Holan, *Mystic*, Fort Lauderdale, FL
Norma Jaget, *Gibson Girl*
Lari Johnson, *Barefoot*
Denise Keary, *Saucey Wench*, Benicia, CA
Judith Kerivan, *Delphinus*
Dee Kermode, *Sweetwater*, Palmetto, FL
Jean Kidd, *Cygne Sauvage*, Pine Island, FL
Sue Klimoski, *Passage*, Miami, FL
Lucie Lee, *Breathless*, Lewes, DE
Marianne Lenfestey, *Air Force Won*, Holly Springs, NC
Lillian Lewis, *Primrose Lane*, Big Rapids, MI
Sue Longacre, *More Mischief*, Annapolis, MD
Barbara Lowenberg, *Last Dance*, Seabrook, TX
Cindi Lutvak, *Rafiki*, Orange Park, FL
Nancy MacNeil, *Tyee*, Derby Line, VT
Damian Maher, *Kittitian*
Dene McCain, *Escape*, St. Helena, SC
Portia McCracken, *Carolina Girl*, Whidbey Island, WA
Lynn McFayden, *Diva*, Wilmington, NC
Barbara McLaughlin, *thirtysomething*, Emmaus, PA
Anne Monnier, *Sea Flat*, Green Cove Springs, FL
Jacki Moraski, *Owlpuss*
Barb Mottice, *Passage*, Half Moon Bay, CA

Phyllis Nass, *Second Venture*, Lodi, NY
Becky O'Cain, Galveston, TX
Jane Owens, *Yolo*, Key West, FL
Pris Pearcy, *Miss Pris*, Corpus Christi, TX
Susie Pierce, *Caribbean Soul*, Mackinaw, IL
Chris Pope, *L'Ambiance*, Green Cove Springs, FL
Pat Poupore, *Sea Yawl*, Rockport, TX
Nina Pratt, *Puffin*, Matunuk RI
Pat Rackl, *Sea Witch*, Buffalo, NY
Gloria Rad, *Emerald Sea*
Karen Rauth, *Sylvia K*, Moore Haven, FL
Terri Robbins, *Patience*, Raleigh, NC
Susan Scott, *Journey*, League City, TX
Marilyn Sharkey, *Corsair II*, Washington, DC
Virginia Shell, *Java*, College Station, TX
Anita Simmons, *Gypsy*, Arnold, MD
Milli Simonis, *Mici*, San Antonio, TX
Skip Skinner, *Skip's Quest*, Edgewater, MD
Robin Slaughter, *Wingin' It*, Corpus Christi, TX
Cindy Snowhite, *Nordic*, Spring, TX
Rachel Sorbie, *Dylan*, Tierra Verde, FL
Denise Stearns, *Knot Enough*, Smithfield, VA
Jan Suckow, *Tapocketa*, Naples, FL
Cass Sutton, *LadyShip*
Betsy Swam, *Mi-Lou XIV*, Baltimore, MD
Lillie Taylor, *Avemar*, Livingston, TX
Ann Thompson, *AnnTicipation*
Joan Tucker, *My Mistress*, Manhattan, IL
Fran Turner, *Turn'er Loose*, Baltimore, MD
Mary Tyner, *Keno*, Titusville, FL
Jeanne VanderMost, *Jean Marie*
Beatriz Vergara, *Siboney IV*, Mississauga, Ontario
Didgie Vrana, Fort Lauderdale, FL
Vi Waldecker, *The Designer*, Washington, DC
Ethan Welch, MD, Rochester, NY
Laura Wenslaff, *Larelle*, Norfolk, VA
Nela Wilems, *Wave Dancer*, Nassau Bay, TX
Barb Wood, *Barberic*, Seattle, WA
Pat Wooldridge, *P & L*, Marathon, FL

The Best Tips from
WOMEN ABOARD®

Contents

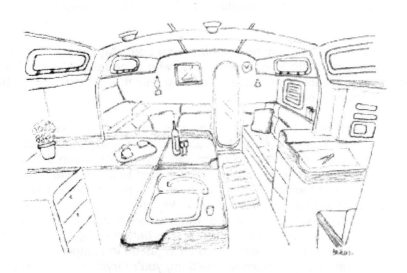

LIVING WITH *WOMEN ABOARD*

"THINGS NOBODY TOLD ME ABOUT LIVING ON A BOAT"

These things wouldn't have affected my decision to live on a boat, but they *were* surprises.

NOISES: Without warning, somewhere in the bowels of the boat, pumps begin to pump. The fresh water pump starts and doesn't stop, because the tank is empty. Fenders and floats moan and groan in the middle of the night. The refrigerator rattles off and on. The stand-alone icemaker makes more noise than the fridge. Breakers click off and things stop running. Waves in an anchorage, combined with a half-empty water tank across the wall from your bed, produce especially awesome sounds. Water laps against things. Debris slaps against the hull. Things go bump in the night. You can't ignore an unfamiliar sound, and in the beginning, you're never really sure where it's coming from.

SCENTS: All boats smell. When they stop smelling new, they smell like diesel, heads, garbage, mildew, and/or fish. Staying ahead of it takes diligence—and cross-ventilation. Sometimes, Stick-Ups. And then there

1

are the smoke and burning smells—they're usually the neighbor's barbeque.

SPIDERS: An arachnophobe can't live on a boat. My theory is: they're wild animals, and wild animals always go where the food is. If we have spiders, we probably don't have something else that we don't want. But they need to stay outside.

COMPLICATIONS: There are ten times as many things to stay on top of as in a house. You can't flush the toilet and always expect it to work—maybe the 12-volt system is down, or the water tank has run dry, or the fresh-water pump is off, or the head switch next to the engine room blower switch got turned off by mistake. Even when docked, you can't always expect the 12-volt lights to work like the ones at home—the house batteries have to be charged, watered, equalized, and sometimes, spoken to nicely. Ditto for the engine starter batteries if you ever want to go anywhere. The refrigerator has to be adjusted to compensate for the room temperature. The switch for the thing you're trying to turn on isn't on the main switch panel—it's over by the helm. Or up on the bridge. Or down in the engine room.

LITTLE SURPRISES: The shower water is 50 degrees hotter when the engines have been running. You don't really have a full starboard water tank—the petcock for the indicator tube was just turned off. Of all the ports that aren't screwed down tight, the one that leaks in the 3 a.m. storm is the one right over your face.

THE VIEW: On the water, the sky, sea, and nearby scenery change in color, tone, and message throughout the day and night, just like the mountains in the desert.

PEOPLE: The good neighbors are the best in the world.

"HOW TO LIVE IN A SMALL SPACE AND GET ALONG"

We don't have many rules aboard the good ship *Keno*. Most are safety-related ones like maintaining cockpit-based watches, wearing safety harnesses—the usual rules most boats enforce to ensure that cruising is a positive experience. However, we do have one rule that we have not come across in discussions with other sailors—the "5 Minute Rule."

Simply put, this rule means that no matter what unpleasantness you have endured from your mate or fellow crew member, you have five minutes to "get over it." You can yell, scream, stomp your feet, get in a huff, or cry. Pick your poison. But you've got five minutes to finish expressing your hurt or discontent and get on with life. The key here is that it's the offending crew that plays the role of caller/timekeeper with the simple statement, "You've got five minutes. Then I'm calling 'time.'" And the timekeeper monitors time as passively as possible, calling out when five minutes have passed. The objective of this process is that it is not a continuation of the conflict, but a step towards returning the tense situation to an "even keel."

It's not always easy to implement, but this rule has added to the joy of cruising aboard *Keno*. After all, it's not as if you can go for a long walk to cool down when you're underway. And believe me, nothing shrinks the size of a boat like an angry or sulking crew member. To permit the atmosphere to be continually charged tends to allow for "anger binges" that significantly disrupt the pleasure of cruising and wastes both fun and work time. To have less than five minutes to "vent your spleen" doesn't give adequate release, especially when the offense cuts deeply. Hence, the five minute time frame.

What makes this rule work is the dedication of *Keno*'s crew to observing it. And the reason *Keno*'s crew is so dedicated to observing this rule is that IT WORKS!

"HONEY, WHERE'S THE..."

One of the more complex job assignments aboard your boat may be the ultimate responsibility for knowing where things are. The answers to the questions: *Do we have it?* and *Where is it stowed?* can make a big difference, whether the problem at hand is an engine repair, an ingredient for a meal, the next bottle of your favorite libation, or out-of-season clothing for an unusual aberration of Mother Nature's.

"Lost On Board" is the punch line of many cruiser jokes, but it ceases to be funny when the needed item is a hose or clamp to repair a leak, gloves or a hat on a nasty, cold day, or even that dab of Grey Poupon for cocktail hour. You'll need a list of every storage space and the items you've tucked in there. Maybe one page in a notebook for each space, one line of the page for each item. In addition you'll need a firm determination to mark off every item used or moved. Does all this sound compulsive? Possibly. Does it remind me

where I've tucked small items of value? Absolutely! Do you need to do the same? Only you can answer that.

Along the same vein, traveling can transform other forms of record keeping: I ask every doctor for a copy of any lab results so that I can have the information at my fingertips should they be needed by a different doctor somewhere down the waterway. Possibly your memory is better than mine, but you'll eventually be asked when and where you had your last tetanus shot, pap smear, mammogram or CBC. After a few years these things may blur in your mind and it's very nice to be able to pull out that fat envelope and retrieve the needed information.

HOW TO ATTACK A MESSY BOAT
(or Cubby / Closet / Lazarette)

Before you even start a project like this, consider each item individually and ask yourself:

1. *Have I used this item in the past year?* If yes, keep it. If no, discard it.
2. *Does it have either sentimental or monetary value to me?* Yes? Keep it.
3. *Might it come in handy someday?* If you answer "yes," but have nothing specific in mind, better put the article into a "Throw-away" or "Give-away" box unless you have someplace to store it. (HA!)

THEN:

Start from the outside in. Take care of the clutter scattered AROUND the cabin before digging into the closet. Starting with the closet first creates a double mess.

Work in one-hour segments. Don't try to do the entire project in one session. When the one hour is up, quit. Schedule another hour, and then another, until the job is finished.

To minimize the mess, arrange four boxes labeled:
- CHARITY
- BELONGS ELSEWHERE
- TRASH and
- DECISION PENDING.

4

Work on a small section at a time. Don't attempt to empty an entire cluttered boat all at once. The resulting chaos will surely set you back or put you off entirely.

STORAGE

Can *any* boat have enough? With many of us bringing aboard "cold weather" clothing and bedding, it's once again time to think about reorganizing those lockers, cubbies, shelves and lazarettes to make room. Here are some hints that might make your life easier.

- Cavernous lockers will be more useful if they're divided into smaller compartments. Quarter-inch plywood can be used to permanently section off locker space. For a temporary "fix," try various sizes of plastic wastepaper baskets or dishpans. Things are kept orderly, and the contents are prevented from shifting and jumbling together when the boats rolls or heels. Pieces of flexible foam can be wedged into odd spaces to prevent rattling while underway.

- Plastic trays on shelves and in drawers keep small items secure. Small bits of office gear, such as stamps, tape, paper clips, and a stapler, can be placed in one tray. Spices can be kept orderly if placed in plastic trays on a galley shelf.

- Rubbermaid makes some inexpensive (under $2 each) drawer organizers that come in 3", 9", 12", and 15" lengths. They also have a rectangular one about 6"x9". All can be made to lock together, and they are great for organizing odd-shaped drawers. One Sea Sister uses them to keep things from sliding around in the odd-shaped cabinet under the sink in her head.

- Plastic containers or trash cans are especially useful for storage in the bilge. These can provide a tidy, efficient arrangement. Plus, if anything leaks or spills, the containers prevent the spillage from going into the bilge.

- Ziploc bags are indispensable. Anything that can be harmed by moisture can be stored in a Ziploc bag. And anything that might damage *something else* should be bagged as well. Tubes of caulk, a partially-used can of oil, grease for the winches, anything gooey, sticky, or messy

5

can be put into its own bag. Be sure to have a variety of sizes of Ziploc bags at hand, especially the 2-gallon size.

- All boxes or closed containers should be labeled. A permanent marker writes on most surfaces. Paper labels last years if covered with Scotch tape.

- If you haven't already done it, take the time to make a list of what is stashed where, and most importantly, keep that list updated. One way is to sketch out the accommodation plan of your boat, showing every storage bin and locker, and assign each locker a number—even numbers to port, odd numbers to starboard. In a notebook, keep a page for each locker, listing EVERYTHING it contains.

- 3M® makes the Marine Recloseable Attachment System, a Velcro-type adhesive of plastic. Will hold down appliances, electronics, or picture frames. Their Fire Barrier Silicone RTV sealant is also good to have.

What seems like a lot of work will end up making your life a lot easier. Imagine what it will be like to locate that long-sleeve, blue T-shirt or those thick, warm socks at a moment's notice. Not to mention not having to answer those endless questions of "Whatever happened to ......?"

OTHER SPACE SAVERS

- SHOE BAGS. Hang one on the back of a hanging locker for socks, underwear, bathing suits, and of course, shoes. They can be cut to as many shoe pockets as you need for an area, then attached with Velcro or screws (backed up with large washers), depending on the weight of the articles being stored.

- One Sea Sister uses four pockets on the removeable lid of the settee that houses her pots and pans. Small plastic lids, can opener, and other small items are stored, taking some of the clutter out of her utensil drawer. This will also work on the insides of doors or in the head.

- VINYL-COATED WIRE RACKS. Added to the inside of access panels can hold extra oil and fuel filters.

- NET BAGS. Indispensable for holding clothing, fruits, vegetables.

6

- HOOKS. Holds keys, coffee mugs, caps, etc. Just be sure that whatever is hanging doesn't swing against a bulkhead. The constant movement will quickly wear through the finish and start to carve a groove.

- CEREAL BOXES. Cut box diagonally from one corner to bottom third of the other side. Reinforce with clear Contact paper. Great for holding magazines and catalogs. Detergent boxes also work well.

- SMALL JARS. Attach lids of small jars (baby food, yeast, etc.) to the underside of shelves. Fill jars with spices or small objects and screw into lids.

- EMPTY TISSUE BOXES. Stuff plastic grocery sacks into empty tissue boxes for neat storage and easy retrieval.

MORE STORAGE IDEAS

- Keep envelopes from gluing shut before their time by placing strips of waxed paper under each flap. The strips can be recycled, so only the initial batch needs to be cut.

- Keep flashlight batteries fresh by storing them in a sealed plastic bag in the refrigerator.

- Photographic film will stay fresh longer if stored in your refrigerator as well.

- Extension cords won't get tangled when stored in a drawer if you wind them and secure them with rubber bands—or slip them into a toilet-paper or paper-towel tube.

- Tack rags won't dry out if stored in an air-tight container. Air-tight storage will also prevent spontaneous combustion of any rags soaked with flammable oils or solvents.

- Trios of metal mesh baskets in graduated sizes would ordinarily be rejected for boat storage because of the material, but the painted ones resist rust for quite awhile. The baskets hang from one hook in a vertical row. Do not allow them to swing freely—among other problems, this causes a series of arch-shaped scratches on the nearest bulkhead. Attach the rim of the lowest basket to the bulkhead with a small screw. Cushion the wire mesh inside with colorful bandannas and use the baskets for fresh fruit or vegetables, potatoes and onions, pet toys, sewing yarn, and other odds and ends.

- Hang FLASHLIGHTS from lanyards on cup hooks handy to companionway and sleeping quarters. You never know when you may need these lights—emergencies never seem to happen during the day

- Storage of extra blankets and bedding: I bought a few zippered cotton pillow protectors (about $3 each) and folded the extra bedding to fit inside. I covered them with pillow shams and tossed them on the settee. The bedding stays fresh, I save space, and the blankets are easily accessible when needed.

- We use several inexpensive drawstring type laundry bags made of nylon to contain and transport laundry to and from the washing machines. One color bag is designated for dark clothing, one for light colors, and one for hot-water-and-bleach. In the winter we even have a separate bag for jeans, as they, and the towels, need to go into the washers first, so that they can get into the dryers soonest. (Only after those two loads are started do I pre-spot and start the lights, which will probably need the least drying time.) It saves time when we arrive at the laundromat, and by throwing the bags in the washing machine with the laundry, they're clean to bring clothes back to the boat.

- To save time when we get back aboard, we also sort dry, folded clothes while they're all spread out on the folding table: my clothes go in one bag, my husband's in another, and general linens (galley and head) in the third. I've even pulled the draw string bags up over the bottoms of clothing taken back to the boat on hangers. That keeps them all together, and the bottom edges clean, as well. Putting away the clean clothes where they belong becomes much easier this way, and the laundry bags then return to their dirty-clothing collecting duties.

- Storage of non-folding bicycles onboard: We use a product called BIKE TIGHT (available at most bike shops, retail, for about $29 each). Made of aluminum, they are mounted on a flat surface (we used a 3 foot piece of 1x5 lumber). The front wheels are removed from the bicycles and the bike is then clamped down. The bikes are securely fastened, but able to be quickly released when needed.

- Concerned about sea spray blanketing your bicycles stored on your deck? Try covering them with a standard cover used for gas grills.

MORE ORGANIZING HINTS

- Extremely well-organized people keep a written record of *every* item on board, alphabetized (and cross-referenced when necessary) on index cards in a file box. For instance, "oil" is subdivided into salad, engine, or lock. Every can of food, every pound of pasta is accounted for, and whenever an item is removed from storage, it is duly noted.

- If you know you wouldn't keep up the file box, try making separate lists for each storage area, including drawers, magazine holders, and locker. Keep the list in a notebook for easy referral.

- Warranties and receipts for boat equipment, electronics, tools, mail orders, etc. are easily retrieved when filed in an accordion file.

- Keep your insurance documents safe. Know when your next premium is due. In some ports, you may be required to show proof of insurance before you are allowed to dock.

- Maintain your address list and update it regularly. Have a fax number for important people on your list. Sometimes it's easier and cheaper to communicate by fax than phone calls.

- Make copies of all valuable papers—passports, vessel registration or documentation, birth certificates, powers of attorney, marriage license, and driver's licenses—and store them in a safe place.

MAKING THINGS STAY PUT
or "THE WONDERS OF CAULK"

To give a glass, plate or candy dish a skid-proof base, run a bead of clear silicon (bathtub) caulk around the bottom, and set it aside, *upside down*, til the silicon 'skins over' (10-15 minutes). Then gently, just momentarily, set the glass right side up on a piece of wax paper or Saran Wrap to flatten the bottom of the caulk so that it is completely level (don't put its full weight down or you'll squeeze out the silicon). Immediately invert the glass again, with the covering in place, and allow to dry, rim side down, overnight. The next day, gently pull off the waxed paper, and you'll have a glass or nicknack that won't skid when the boat rocks. We've used this on the glass globes in which we burn candles, shells that are displayed on shelves, and the bottom of the boat dog's treat jar. These items now need to be secured only in very rough conditions. A small warning: the silicon won't stay in place on dishes used in the microwave.

I even put small blobs of silicon on the feet of our small Christmas tree and put it down, still wet, on our dashboard, gluing it in place. It stayed there all the way across the 'Big Bend' of Florida—lights, ornaments and all, even though we tied down everything else we thought might even think of moving. When Christmas was over, everything cleaned up beautifully—no mess, no fuss, no permanent marks.

When we first moved aboard in December 1990 I didn't want to put screws in the beautifully paneled bulkheads, so I hung my wooden wall clock with silicon caulk and Velcro. After cutting both halves of the Velcro to fit, I used silicon caulk to attach one half to the back of the clock, the other half to the bulkhead. After allowing both to dry for 24 hours, I hung the clock on the wall the next day. The Velcro came loose during the second battery change, but it was quickly reattached the same way. When we sold that boat in 1995, I removed the clock, and carefully peeled the Velcro from the bulkhead. It came away cleanly, leaving no hint that anything had hung there for five years. The same piece of Velcro was reused to hang the clock in our present boat, reattached once again with trusty silicon caulk.

I've used scraps of the frosty shower curtain liner to create matching privacy curtains for the porthole in the shower stall enclosure. With Velcro attached with silicon caulk, my curtain is simple, cheap, removable and easily changed whenever I want. In fact, the frosty shower curtain actually seems to *bring more light into the area*, a bit like the deck prisms you've seen on some sailboats.

MORE HINTS ON MAKING THINGS STAY PUT

- To attach things that have a tendency to slide around on counter tops or shelves, I use *white florist's clay*. Inexpensive, clean and removable, it sticks like crazy, even holding the small electric lamps upright in the worst weather. Hand lotion dispensers stay where you want them, and decorative items are easily moved for dusting around.

- Sliding objects—Rubber material (Scoot Guard) does a great job of making any surface skid-proof. It can be purchased (at Wal-Mart, as well as in boating and hardware stores) in small sections, or by the foot, and easily trims to fit with scissors.

- One Sea Sister had this to say about Velcro: "Besides duct tape, Velcro is the second best thing that must have been invented with boat living in mind. I use it to keep the mounted fire extinguishers in place, to hang the external speakers for the VHF outside the cabin when we're underway, to hold the engine key float while off-duty and in place when underway. (Once, while making a quick step around the helm, I stepped on the key float and broke the starter switch.) My *best use for Velcro* is using it to hold tiny dowel rods in place over the ports. I fashioned curtains by hemming small pieces of cloth and gathering them on the rods. We have privacy in the evenings and yet the curtains go up with the ports because the "V" keeps them snug."

KEEPING MOSQUITOES AT BAY

- For mosquito screens I use nylon screening material (available at most hardware stores.) It's usually 32" wide and you can buy what you need. (Sailrite carries the no-see-um netting.) In addition, I buy 1" "sticky-back" Velcro (about $4.50/yd.) and cut it in half to get maximum usage and to cut the expense. Use the smallest needle you can (#9 or #11) and invisible nylon thread. A mid-length stitch is all you need to attach it to the screen. When using the sticky Velcro, I keep nail polish remover and cotton swabs nearby to clean the needle when it gets gummy.

- Use spring-action curtain rods to mount mosquito screens in doorways and hatches. Cut the material to fit your hatch or door and bind the edges, if desired. Slide the curtain rods inside "sleeves" sewn into the mosquito netting, and position the rods at important points within the opening (i.e., at the top, middle and bottom of the doorway. A hatch would require only two curtain rods). The Sea Sister who engineered this idea had her aft stateroom's doorway cleverly protected in this manner. Using three curtain rods, the mosquito netting snugly fit inside the sliding hatch and doorway.

- To keep no-see-ums from coming through your screens, try spraying the screen material with Pam® (the no-stick spray for pans). This tip comes highly recommended by a fellow cruiser and boat canvas person. Under attack by these beasts, I'd try anything!

- Spray your screens with insect repellent when the mosquitoes are fierce.

TRIED AND TRUE PRODUCTS

- TIME-SAVER TOOLS has what you need to repair and install canvas hardware with a professional look at a reasonable price. Their anvils for setting snaps and grommets slip onto straight-jaw locking pliers and last pretty much forever. They ship UPS direct. Time-Saver Tools Corp., 6806 Indianapolis Blvd., Hammond, IN 64324.

- SAILRITE KITS has a free catalog which gives you a price basis with which to work, and their staff is knowledgeable and helpful. SAILRITE KITS, 305 W. Van Buren St., P.O. Box 987, Columbia City, IN 46725, phone1-800-348-2769, website: www.sailrite.com

- SCREEN PRUF, sprayed on screens, creates a thin, invisible film that protects against sand flies, gnats, and mosquitoes for weeks. It's available at Ace Hardware Stores.

- Use "DOWNY" Dryer sheets to combat the pesky sand gnats so prevalent in places like Georgia. Rub your exposed skin with the dryer sheet and also put one in your hat to keep them out of your hair. Reapply every 30 minutes. (Recommended by the local folks in St. Mary's, Georgia.)

- OFF *SKINTASTIC* SPRAY is a very effective mosquito repellent not just because it WORKS; it isn't greasy!

NATURAL MOSQUITO REPELLENT

2 cups Witch Hazel
1½ tsp. citronella (available at health food stores)
1 Tsp. apple-cider vinegar

Pour ingredients into spray bottle and shake to mix thoroughly. Use as you would any insect repellent, being careful to avoid eyes, nose and mouth.

UPDATING BOAT CUSHIONS

Many women aboard are faced with the challenge of updating a used boat they have purchased, or an older boat they are keeping. Changing the cushion and curtain fabric is generally the quickest and least expensive way to perk up your boat.

- If you select fabric from a home fabric supplier, your interior fabric options are practically limitless. While home fabrics are not specifically designed for outdoor use, choosing them with care and spraying them with a fabric protector (i.e. Scotch Guard) makes them more likely to withstand the use (abuse?) they endure inside a boat.

- Be sure you look for synthetic fibers that resist mildew and rot, such as nylon, acrylic and polyester blends. These materials also have a good memory; in other words, they return to their original good looks after being sat upon.

- Durability is another factor to be considered. Tightly woven fabrics are recommended. Don't forget to test for colorfastness.

- There are special marine fabrics made for interior use, i.e. Sunbrella, manufactured by Glen Raven Mills, Inc. The exterior-grade Sunbrella is also suggested for interior use. It holds up well in wet conditions, is practically waterproof, and still breathes, thus allowing any moisture that was absorbed to disperse. It is very resistant to rot, mildew, and fading. And since it is a woven fabric, it is easier to fit on seats of any kind.

CAUTION! Exterior Sunbrella gives off poisonous fumes if it catches on fire!

- The interior color trend is to select lighter colors for cushions, rather than dark. Choose brighter colors to use on the pillows and to accent bolsters works well, and contrasting piping also adds interest.

- Just as important, if not more so, is the choice of foam to be used in your cushions. There are two main types: open-cell polyurethane and closed-cell. Open-sell polyurethane is the least expensive, all-around foam and comes in varying grades of density. The major problem with it is that it absorbs moisture and this leads to rot. To help control this, wrap foam in a dry cleaner's clothing bag before inserting in the cover.

- "Ultra-open cell" or "reticulated" foam has become available, and this material allows water to drain through quite easily. You might have guessed that it costs more, but it's worth it.

- Closed cell foam is another alternative. It is an excellent choice for boat cushions because it will not absorb water, it floats, and is firmer. It can be used in thinner, less expensive, thicknesses. Although it shrinks a bit over time, its advantages far outweigh its disadvantages, and it's highly recommended for deck cushions.

Choose the best materials you can afford. You won't be disappointed.

SEWING NOTES

Sewing sail or canvas projects without an industrial-type sewing machine can be made easier by using a VINYL ROLLER FOOT (available at most fabric stores for high- or low-shank home machines.) It can be invaluable on rip-stop nylon or Sunbrella. Use V-46 Dabond thread from the Sailrite Kits. It's not as heavy as the V-69 recommended for acrylics, but it's sturdy enough without throwing you into a "tension nightmare." Sailrite also has all kinds of interesting fasteners as well as sewing supplies.

A product called "Sewer's Aid" helps both the bobbin and top threads run more smoothly. It's also handy for stiff or sticking Delrin zippers on enclosures. Keep an emery board in your "sewing stuff" to blunt needles. This allows the thicker-type threads to pass through the material's weave more easily.

14

CARPETING

Be careful when using BERBER CARPET, as it will fray on cut edges and is difficult to bind. One Sea Sister, though, says that she *prefers* berber carpeting on the boat because it doesn't show the dirt, holds salt well, washes clean and looks new even when it's several years old.

Since Lynn owns a sailboat, she buys area rugs and cuts them to fit round corners and narrow spaces. On the cut edges she uses 'LIQUID ROPE WHIPPING' which is a flexible vinyl rope dip available at most boating stores ($5.49 at West Marine). This product is like a thick rubber cement and is designed to permanently seal line ends that would otherwise fray and unravel.

Simply cut the carpet and stroke the cut edges with the Liquid Rope. Allow to dry for a few hours. The carpet will last for years, and survive many washings without fraying. This tip actually works well with any other kind of carpet and fabric too.

BEDDING TIPS

Because we sleep for nearly one-third of our lives, having a comfortable bed definitely ranks high on the list of "Must Haves." Here are some tips we have found useful:

- If you are making your own fitted sheets for your bunks that are odd sized, first make a pattern. If the bunk has at least one right angle, you can do this from measurements only. If not, you will have to trace the bunk onto pattern paper.

- Buy flat sheets only! The sheet size is bigger, and the flat sheet is much easier to work with.

- Buy good quality sheets!!! If you are going through all this trouble, you want them to last!!

- When figuring the size sheet to buy, remember to allow additional length and width for the thickness of the bunk, plus 3" to go under the mattress.

- Blankets usually run much larger than sheets, so that you can get away with buying a smaller size.

- Try to buy anchor band mattress pads. They will spare you the unnecessary added bulk on the sides of the mattress.

- Don't buy comforters...even the expensive ones don't hold up well because the nylon thread ultimately tears loose from the fabric with many washings. Buy quilted bed covers instead. They are thinner, easier to work with, and they are very warm. They also are much easier to wash and dry yourself. But, remember...buy quality!!!

One Sea Sister writes: "My 'marine queen' mattress is an odd shape and an odd size, and it's snugged up tight against the port cabin wall. So making it up was a nightmare, especially after I hurt my back and couldn't wrestle the mattress inside a mattress cover and fitted or strapped sheet. I hated having a messy bed all the time, so I thought about a sleeping bag."

"The sets are outrageously expensive at marine stores (West Marine's Travasak is $259.99), so I kept searching until I found the perfect bag at www.llbean.com. It's their deluxe double camp bag, item #TA24778, which is large enough, has zip out sheets, and is dead easy to make up. And it cost only $149 (and with the LLBean Visa card, there's no shipping cost!)."

"Bean doesn't offer the sheets separately, so I ordered a second set from Slumberjack (1-800-233-6283, ask for the LL Bean Double Deluxe Camp Bag Sheets, #880 LLBV 458 SH @$18.00)."

"Then I found a pretty twin-size quilt, which covers the bed precisely, and a few matching/contrasting pillows to throw on, and voila! I have a beautiful bed in minutes. Nothing has to be tucked in and I can use our sleep pillows, in a pretty, matching set of pillow cases, as a backdrop for the throw pillows."

TIPS ON WINDOW COVERINGS

How do boat manufactures keep those blinds and shades from swaying and clanging against the ports? They use stainless steel wires that are threaded through the existing holders that the cords go through. The wires are secured through the head rail, and at the bottom, below the bottom rail, by screws that are hidden under color-matching caps.

The secret is knowing how taut to make the wire so that it doesn't snap when you tighten the screw. Some people have tried using fishing line, but that stretches, and will lose its effectiveness over time.

WHEN CONSIDERING NEW WINDOW COVERINGS:

Choosing the blind or shade that is right for you will take a little time. Do you:
- Want light?
- Want visibility?
- Want them to open?
- Want them to remain closed?
- Have angles?
- Avoid the angles?
- Want a wide range of color?

And the problems don't end there, for once you decide on the type of window covering, you still have work to do. Things to consider:

- How long do you expect them to last?
- Is the hardware plastic or metal that can rust?
- Can they get wet with salt spray and not stain?
- Can they be washed?
- Will they fade?

Yet another difficult part of this project is the initial measuring. Every part of the space has to be thought out. The blinds are generally square, unless your opening is not and you specify something different.

- Where is the hardware going to be mounted?
- Is there anything in the way of the opening?
- Is there someplace to mount the screws?

Add in the cost of some special tools that are useful and oftentimes necessary to make the installation possible.

Bottom line? This is an extremely difficult do-it-yourself project and the cost of errors can be substantial.

So you decide to hire someone. Good decision. But whom should you call for installation? Are the current suppliers of blinds for the marine industry reliable? These are important questions you need to research.

Cost of the various types of shades also varies. Because of all the different components used, there are many levels of quality. You have to decide what you need, and then do the rest of the research. This is not a one-week project. The other thing to keep in mind is the delivery time. The higher the quality of the blind, the longer the delivery time. Figure anywhere from 4 to 6 weeks.

MORE DECORATING TIPS

- Use furniture-weight Sunbrella for Roman shade-type curtains. It uses less fabric, is more efficient coverage, is fade resistant, and is easy to launder.

- Snap curtains, which are a simulated Roman shade, use less fabric than standard boat curtains, can be made with Sunbrella, and need not be lined. AND look neat, wash easily, and require little hardware to hang.

- A VINYL TABLE CLOTH protects the table and makes all dishes non-skid!

- If you have two average size bunks, you may be able to get two bottom sheets out of one king flat. NEVER buy fitted sheets when making sheets to fit your bunks!!!

- Avoid putting the hard side of the Velcro (the hook) in a place where it is likely to fray any fabric. Because of the hook, it will grab onto any small threads, and begin to break down the fabric.

- When using MARINE ZIPPERS on cushion covers, make sure that the zipper runs part way along each side of the cushion wherever possible, as well as across the back, to easier removal when laundering.

- Speaking of zippers, one Sea Sister who was experiencing sticky zippers on the dodger was told by a few neighbors to try LIP BALM WITH SUNSCREEN to coat the zipper and protect it from ultra-violet rays.

18

What a great idea! Now she keeps several balms on board, some for the crew and some for the equipment.

- One Sea Sister wrote: "COTTON LACE MADE PERFECT NO-SEW CURTAINS for our portholes. This cream-colored, 12" wide lace has openings in the design along one edge that are just right for threading onto a wooden dowel. I threaded two 18" long panels onto an 18" stained and varnished dowel for each porthole. Stitch Witchery keeps the cut edges from unraveling. I screwed two brass cup hooks to the ceiling panels, tied the dowel to the cup hooks with narrow satin ribbons, and adjusted the height so the lace just touches the ceiling."

BEING ABOARD IN COLD CLIMATES

- INSULATE ALL LOCKERS OPENING TO THE HULL to eliminate condensation that can dampen your clothes. Line lockers with good-quality foam padding with the vapor barrier (used with indoor/outdoor carpeting), making sure that the vapor barrier is kept towards the locker door. Liquid Nails does wonders; just make sure the hull surface is *completely* dry. Remember to include the overhead of any locker that is exposed to the walk-around deck.

- DAMP RID CRYSTALS reduce humidity to a level which prevents the growth of mildew and prevents odor. The crystals—calcium chloride— are also marketed as "Damp Away" and "No Damp" at marine stores. But DAMP RID can be found at grocery stores, and drug and discount stores and is much less expensive.

- ENSOLITE (which can be found in sporting good stores) helps eliminate mildew in mattresses. If your bed is regular-size, you might want to order directly from the company (North by Northeast, Pawtucket, Rhode Island, 800-556-7262.)

- One Sea Sister's biggest breakthrough in the condensation problem was discovering ETHEFOAM SHEETING. It is white and pliable and comes in different thicknesses, cut to your desired length. She bought a number of different thickness of it wholesale from an insulation specialty warehouse. Although gluing it to your hull is recommended, she cut it to fit very snuggly so it stayed in place. Next to the hull she put the 1/2" ethefoam, lining all of her lockers and bins. She had just started her business and had lots of paperwork. With ethefoam in the lockers she could keep paperwork next to the hull and it stayed as dry as if it had been in a house! Now THAT was a miracle!

- An alternative to having a damp mattress is to ENCLOSE IT IN A ZIPPERED PLASTIC CASE, which can be bought at discount and department stores.

- HEAT-SHRINK can be applied to window frames to 1) cut down on condensation, and 2) to cut down on drafts. 3M® has been recommended as the best since the double-sided adhesive tape can be easily removed in the spring.

- The same heat-shrink can also be applied around hatches and doorways in aft-staterooms. One neighbor goes a step further and first cuts a piece or two of styrofoam to insert in the hatch, and THEN applies the heat-shrink. Cold drafts are reduced dramatically.

- FLANNEL SHEETS are soft, cozy and warm—makes your bunk *so* comfy, you will probably find it hard to get up in the morning! Try *making* blankets from polar fleece rather than buying already-made ones. By making your own, the size of the blanket will fit your bunk much better, AND, you can choose a color that will coordinate with your interior.

- AN ELECTRIC MATTRESS PAD was whole-heartedly endorsed by a Sea Sister who had endured 10 Washington, DC winters! Note that this is an electric PAD, not an electric blanket!

- KEEP A CUP OF WATER IN YOUR ENGINE ROOM and dip your finger in from time to time. This will give you an idea of how cold it really IS down there. Be aware if ice begins to form on the top. Further steps may need to be taken to prevent any engine damage that will occur if it gets too cold.

- Pour cheap GIN or VODKA IN YOUR WATERTANK to prevent freezing. A quart of booze, diluted with 40 gallons of water, can hardly be tasted.

- To keep your canvas as dry as possible, try saturating your outdoor canvas, including bimini, with THOMPSON'S WATER-SEAL ULTRA WATERPROOFER. This works *magic*! It passes industry standards for water repellency and resistance to wind-driven rain. Although it can be

20

applied several different ways, we found that using a garden "pump up" sprayer is simple and very effective.

- Be sure to KEEP AN EYE ON YOUR ELECTRICAL USAGE! When your heating units are running, be aware of the load that cooking appliances place on your electrical supply! Replacing those shorepower systems can be expensive, not to mention the potential of an electrical fire. Be careful!

- "We bought some "mechanic's suits" at Wal-Mart that were quite helpful. They are insulated, pretty cheap, and you can zip them up over all your other layers of clothes. Goodwill and other thrift stores always seem to have a goodly supply of real wool sweaters—I even found nice soft lambswool—and pants. Who cares what they look like—they'll be covered up and you'll toss away all but one of them when you reach Florida anyway.

DEALING WITH CONDENSATION, MOLD, AND MILDEW

Condensation is a constant challenge that, as long as your boat is in cooler climates, can only be minimized, not dealt with "once and for all." There are ways to battle it:

- You can control excess dampness by using *dehumidifier crystals* (Damp Rid, No Damp, Dri-Z-Air) which can be purchased at marine stores and places like K-Mart, Target, or Wal-Mart. The crystals absorb the moisture from the air, which then drips into a container. Periodic emptying of the container and replenishment of the crystals is all you need to do to control moisture in lockers, settees and cabinets.

- Charcoal briquettes or cat litter in foil or plastic containers also absorbs moisture and can be placed in lockers, under bunks, etc.

- Goldenrod™ dehumidifiers run on 110V and can be hung in closets and heads to control moisture.

- Seats and bunks may absorb condensation that drips down the hull, resulting in cold, uncomfortable seating and a constant case of mildew. To combat this problem, put squares or strips of air-conditioner filter material under the cushions. The thickness of the A/C filter raises the

21

seat or bunk, and the material itself allows air to circulate, keeping the underside dry.

- If copper tubing is led through clothing lockers, cover it with foam rubber pipe insulation. By doing so, condensation won't drip from the metal to your clothing, creating a favorable environment for mold and mildew and causing hard-to-remove stains.

- *Air circulation/ventilation* is paramount to minimizing condensation. For instance, running heaters or fans, keeping lockers, settees and closets open for part of the day, installing solar or mushroom vents, etc.

- Realize that moisture-producing activities, such as showering aboard and cooking foods like pasta, will compound your problem.

- Protect items that are stowed close to the hull, especially towels, clothing, toilet paper, paper towels and the like. Zippered plastic storage bags, 2-gallon Ziploc® bags, etc. can help.

- Use of a chlorine solution (¼ - ½ cup per gallon of water) cleans mildew from painted surfaces and discourages its return. REMEMBER TO WEAR RUBBER GLOVES AND MAKE SURE THE BOAT IS WELL VENTILATED WHEN YOU'RE CLEANING.

- Baking soda cleans most surfaces, and is easier on the hands and nose.

- Lemon juice or a mixture of baking soda and water, followed by a few hours of sunshine, often removes mildew stains on clothing or other fabrics.

- Try using straight vinegar. One Sea Sister said that the results seem to last longer than when she used the chlorine solution, without any of the fumes!

- If mildew has attacked the paint on the interior of your boat, don't try to hide it by covering it with paint. The paint will just flake off as the mildew continues to grow. First, wash the surface thoroughly with a chlorine bleach solution, and let it dry completely before attempting to paint. Add a mildew-inhibitor to the new paint. (For information on M-1 Additive, contact BOATEK at 800-336-9320.)

FUN IN THE YARD or "HOW TO LIVE ABOARD UP IN THE AIR WHILE IN THE BOAT YARD"

One Sea Sister in the Florida Keys was hauled out for several months in 1999. She wrote to say she is "trying to be creative" in using her spare time. She has painted and recarpeted all her cupboards, using indoor/outdoor carpet runners, cutting pieces to size. Faith says they're fairly cheap and have a rubber backing.

Another project is updating her catalog supply. Besides *Cruising World's* catalog, and of course, West Marine, Defender, Boater's World, etc., Faith sends away for anything that <u>might</u> be useful: RV supplies, camping, fishing, or hunting catalogs (like Cabela's). Many times the products are <u>exactly</u> the same but since they don't say "marine," the prices are more reasonable.

She advises: "When making major purchases, it's smart to be armed with general pricing and some options of what is "out there." Even dinnerware and flatware, pots and pans, carpets, light fixtures, foul weather gear and binoculars can be ordered through catalogs. And since most of the suppliers are in a state other than yours, there's no sales tax! "We pay 7½% here (Florida Keys). On a $600 item that's $45—shipping is only $8-10. The difference is a "pizza night" for me!"

Here are some more tips to "help you stay sane when your time comes:"

- Assemble all the supplies, paint, and new parts that you anticipate needing *before* going to the yard (there will be plenty of *unanticipated* needs to keep you busy running errands once you're there).

- Anticipate restroom needs. This particular Sea Sister makes an effort to curtail those middle-of- the-night needs that otherwise would require a drafty trip across the dark yard to the usually none-too-clean yard head (punctuated by that shaky trip up and down the ladder), by acquiring a sturdy bucket (ideally with a lid and a seat) and some type of port-a-potty chemical (or pine oil).

- Stock up on paper plates, bowls, cups etc., to keep dishwashing to a minimum. There are so many times when you cannot let water drain out because the hull needs to be kept dry.

- Put a large plastic bowl or dish pan in each sink for the times we forget.

- Plan quick and simple meals, i.e. cereal, sandwiches and soups. The best part is the captain soon gets tired of these so out we go!

- Get satellite TV.

- Resign yourself to TV dinners. You can't wash dishes unless you want to turn yourself into a "ladder martyr."

- Forget your decks that you usually keep so clean. Attend to them after you're back in the water. However, if you see a blue dust film from someone else's grinding, clean it off immediately with foaming bathroom cleaner and a damp rag. Otherwise, it will stain permanently.

- Realize that the boatyard employees are being paid by the hour. If you have questions about work you're doing and need advice, ask the boatyard manager.

- Get written, signed estimates.

- Wear the masks and protective clothing that is suggested.

- Don't shortcut anything below the waterline.

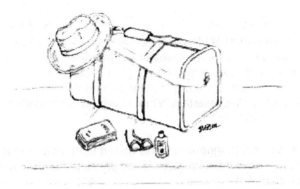

HAVING GUESTS ABOARD

Sharing life afloat with friends and family gives them a chance to experience boat life, while giving you a chance to see through "fresh" eyes. There are many aspects of boating that we take for granted, but the uninitiated will need very specific instructions. Remember that this first day of boating might lead to a lifetime of pleasure for your guests or a day of hell that might prevent them from ever going boating again. Please try and make it a pleasant experience for them and for yourself by preparing them for the trip.

REMEMBER: Don't get in too much of a hurry or try to cover too much ground in a limited time span, and don't allow schedules to override your good sense when the weather is bad! Going because you just 'have to get there' to meet some schedule, when your gut feeling (if you'll listen to it) tells you that you shouldn't, is a good way to get yourself and your boat knocked around. Try to plan ahead for weather delays, and keep yourselves, *and especially guests*, prepared with alternate, backup plans.

- The one characteristic boat guests need most is *adaptability*, for their sake AND yours. Uptight and narrow-minded types will not enjoy their stay in the least (suggest a hotel room for these people!)

- Insist that guests' first visits be short. First-timers will have enough to adjust to (space, water/electricity management, boat movement) without prolonging the experience.

- Don't be afraid to have kids aboard. It could be a great learning experience for them. Get—or borrow—a few kid-things to have on board: coloring books, crayons, drawing paper, playing cards, games.

- Send your guests a list of titles—or actual books—of the places they're coming to see. Do this several weeks before their visit. Ask *them* what they'd like to do with their time. You might not be able to do it all, but at least you won't get the standard answer of "I don't care," or "It's up to you" in response to the question "What do you want to do?"

- Send your guests a list of clothes and supplies they'll need. Tell them to bring casual clothes (suggest mix-and-match outfits), and maybe ONE good outfit to wear. If doing laundry is not possible on the boat, forewarn them of that also.

- Allow ONE bag—soft luggage or duffel—per person. No exceptions.

- Explain ahead of time that they may have to live out of the bag (empty drawers and closets not available.)

- Remind them about the kind of shoes they should wear (deck shoes, ordinary sneakers.)

- On the before-they-come list, explain the boater's cultural experience of *marina showers*. Have them bring a transportable shower kit, stress *plastic containers* rather than bottles or jars, and remind them to bring flip-flops for shower floors.

- Take some time to tell to your guests:
⇒ How to use the head;
⇒ The location and use of fire extinguishers and PFDs;
⇒ How to use the stove;
⇒ How to make a simple call on the VHF;
⇒ Where the first aid kit is located.

- Put together a GUEST KIT for your friends' arrival, to include:
⇒ a bottle of sunscreen; a visor, to shade head, eyes, and nose;
⇒ eyeglass straps, because they probably won't bring spare glasses;
⇒ a personal log (small notebooks will do) and encourage them to keep a daily record of daily events and impressions. If you compare notes the day before they leave, you may find it funny and sometimes fascinating at how different the logs can be!

- A few lightweight white cotton shirts and some drawstring-waist pajama-type pants are handy to have on board. That way, when the guest who "never" burns begins turning the color of a lobster, you can loan him the sun-bouncing outfits to wear until he heals.

- If you don't have enough pillows, consider inflatables. Or, you can stuff a pillowcase with beach towels, sweatshirts, and heavy sweaters.

- Guests often ask what they can do. Give them options such as cooking, doing the dishes, or a small boat-repair project. They'll feel as though they're making a contribution to the team-effort!

- If you're obsessed with organization and neatness, remember that for some, clutter is a way of life. Accept the fact that this is only a temporary situation, and try your best to ignore the things that might upset you. Everyone will have a better time.

- Allow some time for separate activities. You might recommend something on shore that you've already seen and that they might enjoy. Loan them your bikes or direct them to local transportation.

- It can be a lot of fun to entertain guests who are new to the boating lifestyle. Remember your early days aboard so that you can prepare your guests as much as you can.

- Sharing your home and your lifestyle will be a real eye-opening experience to your first-time guests. Think of ways to make the most of the time your guests will be on board. Then enjoy!

In addition to providing your guests with a "guest bag" which might contain items such as small soaps, snacks and maybe crayons and a coloring book for the younger set, you might want to prepare them for their trip with a "Welcome Aboard" letter which will make their stay a pleasant one for everyone by laying the ground rules from the very beginning.

Some of the things to initiate your guests to boating in general and your boat in particular are:

Coming Aboard – Where to step, hold...through transom door off swim platform or (up steps) over the side and up/down to the deck. This becomes even more critical if you are not at floating docks.

Clothing and Luggage – Whether for the day or weekend, only bring one soft luggage per person and soft soled, non-marking shoes. Bring fewer clothes than you think you'll need, but prepare for warm/cool/wet weather conditions.

Medication – Bring regular medication even though you think you will be back before you need another dose… weather or other boating disasters might prevent you from getting back at the anticipated time.

Personal Items – Even though you might have a generator or shore power, those 1200-watt hair dryers might spell "overload" on a boat. Remind guests to consider non-electric shavers, curling irons (see p. 41), etc.

Bathroom (head) – Since toilets do not operate like those at home, show them how to operate the heads before you leave the dock and remind them that only those things that were eaten first should be put down the head. With limited drinking and hot water, remind your guests to conserve.

Alcohol – Even though your guests are not at the helm, too many cold beers on a hot day might lead to accidents.

Emergencies – Where are the life preservers? How do you put them on? When? What are you going to do in a MAN OVERBOARD SITUATION? After an emergency happens is not the time for instruction.

Fire – Discuss what to do, where to go, the location of the fire extinguishers and how to use them.

Smoking & Alcohol – Will you allow them on your boat and under what circumstances can they be used?

* * *

Some simple instructions can make the day a pleasant boating experience for everyone. A sample "Welcome Aboard!" letter follows. Feel free to modify and/or copy it for your own use.

28

WELCOME ABOARD SUGGESTIONS FOR OUR GUESTS

Since we want you to enjoy your trip aboard our boat, the following is a partial list of things to remember as you are preparing for our trip. We will show and explain everything necessary when you arrive, but please review this list to make your stay an enjoyable one.

The purpose of this preliminary list of suggestions is only intended to assist our guests in being able to enjoy their time aboard. We will explain other items as we tour the boat on your arrival. We look forward to spending time with you aboard our first love, our boat.

Captain and Crew

1. **Coming Aboard** – If you are coming aboard or are departing from the boat, you may open the transom door, step on swim platform and step up/down to/from the dock. You may also go up the two steps on either side of the cockpit and step on the "rubber pad" on the wooden cap rail and step on the dock. If we are not at a "floating dock", please ask for assistance if you need help getting on or off the boat.

2. **Life Preservers/Cushions** – Life preservers and cushions are located on the flybridge in yellow vinyl bags marked "Life Preservers". All children under 10 years old are required to wear one at all times. In case of heavy weather, all passengers will be required to wear one.

3. **Painted or Varnished Surfaces (Bright work)** - Please be careful with all painted or varnished surfaces by not placing items with metal or hard bottoms on these items. It takes a lot of work to get the wood to look this good!

4. **Clothing and Luggage** – Please bring only one soft-sided bag per person and soft soled, non-marking shoes. Bring fewer clothes than you think you'll need, but prepare for warm/cool/wet weather conditions. We will provide bath and beach towels plus bedding.

5. **Medication** – If you think you will get "sea sick", please take your anti-nausea medication as early as possible before you leave home or leave the dock. Bring regular medication even though you think you will be back before you need another dose… weather or other boating problems might prevent you from getting back at the anticipated time. No illicit drugs please.

6. **Personal Items** – Even though we have electricity aboard at the dock and at anchor, 1200-watt hair dryers can mean overload on the electrical system. Please bring non-electric shaver, curling iron, etc.

7. **Bathroom (head)** – Since the toilets do not operate like those at home, we will show you how to operate them before you leave the dock. Please remember that only those things that have been eaten first should be put down the head. Toilet paper must be put in the trashcan next to the toilet in the Ziploc bag.

8. **Showers** – With limited drinking and hot water, please conserve. We ask that when taking a shower, you wet down, turn the water off, soap up and rinse off. Dry in the shower, clean hair from the lint trap and leave the shower clean. You will be given your own towels and wash cloths. Please hang them where indicated.

9. **Alcohol** – Even though you are not at the helm, too many cold beers on a hot day can lead to accidents. No alcohol will be allowed until we are at the pier or at anchor at the end of the day.

10. **Refrigeration** – The refrigerator in our kitchen (galley) is for food only. Cold drinks can be found in the cooler next to the wet bar. Ice can be found in the ice maker in the same location.

11. **Emergencies** – Many different types of emergencies can occur on a boat... some are more hazardous to one's health than others. If you see a problem, please tell the captain immediately. Shout loudly since the sound of the engines can drown out your voice.

12. **Overboard** – If someone falls overboard, immediately begin shouting "Overboard! Overboard!" and point to the person in the water. Throw any deck cushion, life ring, or empty cooler toward the person. We will immediately turn the boat around to retrieve the person.

13. **Fire** – There are fire extinguishers aboard the boat inside the cabin at the lower helm, in the kitchen, in your guest room, and on the flybridge. In the event of a fire, sound the alarm and move aside. Smoking is not permitted anywhere aboard the boat.

14. **Blocking Access** – Please keep your possessions in your bag in your quarters. Companionways must always remain unblocked.

The captain and crew must move quickly under certain circumstances. Please stand aside and do NOT try to assist unless asked. We can do it quicker than try to stop and explain how you can help in a difficult situation.

15. **Equipment** – Please do not use any equipment on the boat unless you ask first and are given instructions on how to use the item. Even though many systems duplicate those at home, they do not operate the same way, break more easily, and cost much more to repair.

16. **Clean Up** – Due to limited space in the galley, we prefer to take care of clean up and dish washing. We ask that you enjoy yourself during your stay.

17. **Weather** – Even though we have navigation equipment that allows us to "see" in many difficult weather situations, a rough ride is not pleasant for anyone. Therefore, we are not always able to keep to a set schedule. Please be aware that we might not return to the dock at the anticipated time due to unforeseen circumstances. Please make allowances for this situation.

18. **Swimming/Snorkeling/Diving** – We will tell you when it is safe to go into the water. Please remember never to dive into unfamiliar water. We have air mattresses and other water toys to play with. Please, no scuba diving unless you are certified.

19. **Dinghy** – You will be invited to use the dinghy for exploring, short trips and fishing after a few minutes of instruction. Always tell the captain before you leave. You will be required to take a hand-held VHF, water bottle, and first aid kit, in addition to being asked to wear a life jacket. Be cautious of your wake near other boats and bathers. Please make sure the dinghy is securely tied up or beached before leaving it.

20. **Entertainment** – Prior to your trip, we will discuss where we are going and what we can do when we get there.

21. **Expenses** – We will not allow any of our guests to share in any operational costs of the trip. Unless discussed beforehand, we will provide all food and beverages. We do ask that everybody pay for his or her own personal expenses.

22. **Pets** – Even though we love them, please leave them at home.

HOLIDAYS ABOARD

Do your family and friends lament that they have NO idea what to get for you for birthdays and Christmas, since you've got such limited storage space? Here's a list of things that you just might need, and they might not have thought of:

- PAPERBACK BOOKS are always welcome. Best sellers and practical boating books especially.

- A new TAPE or CD from a favorite artist. Instructional language tapes, too, if the boat is headed for foreign ports.

- WALKMANS or DISCMANS (or variations thereof), that can be worn while working on the brightwork, standing watch alone, or relaxing.

- BATTERIES

- VIDEO TAPES: recent-releases, family events, cruising guides, tutorials, documentaries.

- Exotic blends of coffee, chocolate, rum-soaked cakes, and the like.

- A carefully thought-out liquor locker.

- Note paper or stationery bearing the boat name. Stamps.

- 100% cotton *anything*! T-shirts that say unusual things or those celebrating special events, like the Whitbread Around the World Race or the America's Cup. Naturally, woolens will be welcomed farther north.

- Stocking stuffers that include things like wire ties, 1 lb. of stainless steel screws, and an assortment of crimp fittings for wire splies, and airtight food containers.

- Gift certificates from large mail-order houses for marine supplies, clothing, foodstuffs.

THE 12 TIPS OF CHRISTMAS ABOARD

1. A small cache of Christmas decorations, clothing, and music is well worth the valuable storage space. Trees should be squishable. Ornaments should be small, non-breakable, and non-corroding.

2. A hand-held tape player with extra batteries allows for unlimited hours of Christmas music without wearing down the ship's batteries.

3. Green plastic twist ties fasten lights to lifelines quickly, don't bleed dye onto the deck, and can be removed easily to get underway or during bad weather.

4. Pack recipes and hard-to-find ingredients necessary to prepare traditional family favorites.

5. Check local customs concerning holiday celebrations. There's no mail, half-price sales, or groceries in British colonies on December 26th; it's Boxing Day.

6. Carry U.S. stamps for mailing Christmas cards with folks flying back to the States.

7. Buy, wrap, and mail Christmas gifts to family and friends before leaving home. The cost of overseas postage can be shocking.

8. Ask family members to stock up on paper & bows during after-Christmas sales. Those items are hard to find in July.

9. Duty charges will be assessed on gifts that family members mail to you in foreign countries.

10. Colored tissue paper and a roll of ribbon require less storage space than wrapping paper & bows.

11. Families chartering for the holidays may wish to wrap photographs of bulky gifts and leave the presents themselves waiting at home.

12. Save memories. Photograph and camcord holiday activities. Buy or create a special ornament each year. Tape local Christmas music. Keep a holiday cruising journal.

WHILE ABOARD, REMEMBER TO TAKE CARE ....OF _YOURSELF_!

From Greek mythology comes the story of Achilles, foremost hero of the Trojan War, who was slain by Paris after being wounded in the only vulnerable part of his body, his heel. Actually, his tendon. The story is the basis for a term in the English language, _Achilles heel_, defined in the dictionary as "a seemingly small, but actually mortal, weakness".

When we were docking _AnnTicipation_ in Pensacola in a substantial crosswind on Friday, the thirteenth of June (no kidding), I pushed off the side deck to get over the coach roof to the other side of the boat, and heard and felt my Achilles tendon snap. I was in pretty good physical condition, and we had been cruising and tying up in a variety of marinas for four weeks. I just pushed off with my right foot only a little more aggressively than usual. The result: a completely severed tendon!

My surgeon, who is a specialist in sports-related injuries, told us that although Achilles tendon ruptures could be found throughout the sports world, the problem occurs quite often among boaters. The reason: in spite of

34

what we may think, most boaters lead fairly sedentary lives, punctuated by occasional bursts of high level physical activity which puts a strain on unconditioned muscles, ligaments, tendons, etc. He advised us (and asked that tell our boating friends) to make a point of stretching our Achilles tendons as part of our daily exercise routine.

My therapist recommends standing back from a solid support and lean on it with your forearms, your head resting on your hands. Bend one leg and place your foot on the ground in front of you leaving the other leg straight, behind you. Slowly move your hips forward until you feel a stretch in the calf of your straight leg. Be sure to keep the heel of the straight leg on the ground and your toes pointed straight ahead. Hold an easy stretch for 30 seconds. Then, slightly bend the back knee keeping the foot flat and hold for 15 seconds.

Another good exercise for your ankles, Achilles tendons, groin, lower back and hips, is to place your feet shoulder width apart and pointed out at a 15° angle, heels on the ground, bend your knees and squat down, holding this position for 30 seconds.

For many of us, exercising is a chore. In the case of the Achilles tendon, an ounce of prevention is worth a ton of the cure.

PERSONAL TIPS FROM SEA SISTERS

- When you buy coated elastic bands by the package, wrap all of them around the handle of your hairbrush. You won't have to go searching for the package or the loose bands.

- Remember that scalps can get sunburned, too. Apply sunblock to the part of your hair with a Q-tip if you expect to be out in the sun without a hat.

- Wash combs and brushes by putting them in a nylon bag and tossing them into the washing machine.

- To eliminate the annoyance of water running down your arms while you wash your face, wear wrist sweatbands.

- Put a pinch of powdered alum (available at your grocer's spice section or the drugstore) into skin fresheners, toners or astringents, then shake and apply to skin. Large pores should be less noticable.

- To remove tar from the bottom of your feet, nothing works better than toothpaste. Tar comes right off.

- Another remedy for beach-tar is baby oil.

- If the screws on the bows of your glasses tend to work loose, touch the top of them with a drop of clear nail polish.

- Foam plastic egg cartons, tucked into rubber boots, keeps them from flopping over in the bottom of the oily locker.

- Shoe organizers, which can be purchased just about anywhere, can be cut to fit any hanging locker (they Velcro-fit around the pole). With limited cubby space, this is great for bras, underwear, socks, etc., that tend to get lost. And shoes!

- An alternative deodorant: Try a crystal rock that you can buy at a health food store and other places you buy deodorant. You have to wet the stone and rub it on wet. This product kills the bacteria that causes the body odor, and yet has no smell of its own. It will still allow you to sweat, but with no odor.

- Striking a match will instantly eliminate unsavory smells in the head.

- It used to be that telemarketers would only call around dinner-time. Now they call at all hours of the day. Tired of it? Florida residents might be interested to know that statutes provide that consumers may register their telephone numbers in a "No Sales Solicitation," published by the Florida Department of Agriculture and Consumer Services. Telemarketers are prohibited from placing a sales solicitation call to any number on this list, as well as any unlisted or unpublished telephone number. There is an initial fee of $10.00 for the first year of this service, and $5.00 for every year thereafter. But it's worth it! Call 800-435-7352 in the state of Florida. If you live elsewhere, look in your White Pages telephone book, or contact your state capitol's Division of Consumer Services.

- If your boat has two heads, consider making them "his" and "hers". There's such a thing as too much togetherness in a head that is 4' x 5', including the shower. In our case, I use the one on the other side of the salon, opposite the master stateroom, since I'm usually the last to bed and earliest up in the morning. Since we have a few portholes that aren't covered, this requires always having a robe or sweat suit stationed at each end of the route!

- Planning on salt water showers in the Bahamas this year? I've used plain old Suave shampoo as a liquid bath soap and found that it foamed very nicely in salt water. Not only did I wash myself with it (I did indulge myself with a fresh water rinse—mainly to keep the salt water out of the towel), but I also washed Ninfa, the boat dog, with Suave in salt water, and discovered that a salt water rinse worked just fine. She smelled and looked great, and her fur felt clean and soft.

- Those pretty net bath sponges are great for any bath or shower. Not only do they seem to make any soap lather up much more than any wash cloth I've ever tried; they also dry completely between showers, and never seem to get funky smelling!

- Did you know that the insulated bags used by ice cream stores to transport ice cream cakes are about the same size as a Sun Shower? And that DAIRY QUEEN offers them for sale? What does this mean? It means that your Sun Showers, containing the water that has been heated throughout the day, can be placed inside the insulated bag and will stay warm for your bath later on that evening! (Make a hole in the bottom seam of the fabric bag for the shower hose to come through, if you'd like.) The bag is also useful for toting ice to the boat.

- One Sea Sister writes: "I have to tell you about a new product from Velcro called GET A GRIP. It's the hook and loop sides stuck back-to-back. Cut a piece any length to secure power cords, line, etc. and it's a done deal! You can create life-line "hold-ups" effortlessly. It seems this product has countless uses."

- A Sea Sister who works from home writes: "We have a space crunch on counter space in our salon because it is all taken up by my computer equipment. So we've been limited to a tiny (4" screen) portable that sits wherever there's a little spot for it at the time. We had the bright idea of getting a card for the computer that plays TV on the 17" desktop monitor.

The one we got is called "WinTV" and we are quite pleased with it. It isn't quite full-screen or Sony Trinitron quality, but it is quite viewable from across the room, which was our objective. It accepts cable, antenna, and VCR input. We got the stereo version, $99.99 at CompUSA. The mono version was about $20 less."

- Living aboard has its advantages but I miss my fresh-cut flowers. I recently went into a gift store and discovered the "Wonderful Windowvase"! It is a transparent flexible plastic "vase" that mounts on to a window, glass door, morrow, or fiberglass wall with suction cups. You mount it, fill it with water and add fresh cut flowers. Voila! A non-breakable, non-knock-overable, perfect way to keep flowers on board without fear of broken glass. There are four sizes and shapes and they all can be easily cleaned. I love it. When ashore, it hangs on the sliding glass door or front storm door at the condo. These vases are made by "Humans," in Vancouver, Canada, phone 604-731-0503, fax 604-731-0585.

- Tap Lights ($19.95 for a set of 6). These are battery operated lights that can be set or hung in dark places, such as hanging lockers, lazarettes, or heads. They're even reputed to be weather-proof so, theoretically, they can be used on deck or dockside. Order by calling 1-800-641-7373.

DOUBLE-DUTY ITEMS include:

- BETADINE: First aid. 3 Tablespoons per 1 quart water as a douche. Disinfectant for dishes if one of the crew is sick.

- FACIAL MASQUE: Use as a drawing salve for splinters. Also for fire ant bites.

- WITCH HAZEL ON COTTON BALLS: Relieves sun-glared eyes, the itch of bug bites, sunburns, or just to help cool you off.

- BLEACH: Laundry. Also removes stains from fiberglass. Replaces chemicals in macerater's head treatment system. The Suffolk County, New York Department of Health recommends using 6 oz. bleach per 10-gallon holding tank. They feel this is kinder to the environment because bleach doesn't contain the formaldehyde, copper and other heavy metals the standard treatments do.

- WISK: Good for cleaning fiberglass decks. Also for bleaching out teak.

- VINEGAR: For sunburned skin. Gives relief and won't dry out your skin. Also soothes insects bites.

- TOOTHPASTE: For burns, especially *steam burns*.

- Pour HOUSEHOLD AMMONIA or use MEAT TENDERIZER on jelly fish stings to neutralize the poison. For spider bites and bee stings, make a paste of meat tenderizer or MSG and water. Cover the bite or sting with the mixture and allow to dry.

- MOIST TOWELETTES/CHUBS/WET WIPES: When trying to conserve water, "luxuries" like washing your hands as often as you might like are often frowned upon. Keep these on hand to freshen up. After cleaning your hands or face, extend their usage by wiping down fixtures, the bathroom sink, the commode seat, whatever! Wipes containing CLOROX are now available.

- Stop bleeding and disinfect minor wounds with MCCORMICK/ SCHILLING ALUM. Help clot a minor cut by dabbing on M/S Alum. Alum is both an antiseptic and a pain reliever that can prevent the infection from getting worse.

- Pour REALEMON on a cut or apply with a cotton ball.

- Soothe a burned tongue with DOMINO SUGAR. Sprinkle a dash of Domino Sugar on your tongue if it has been burned by hot soup, tea, or coffee.

- Treat minor burns with BETTY CROCKER POTATO BUDS. Mix Buds with enough water to make a thick paste, and apply to the burn. Or, apply wet LIPTON TEA BAGS directly to the burn, or secure in place with gauze. Or, try Miracle WHIP. Rub it into the burn. Let it set, then wipe off. Or, apply SUEBEE HONEY to the injury. Honey is hygroscopic and absorbs water, creating an environment in which disease-producing micro-organisms, deprived of their moisture, cannot live. Or, APPLY PREPARATION H to the burn and cover with a fresh sterile bandage every day.

- Alleviate an earache caused by a cold, sinus infection, or allergy with WRIGLEY'S SPEARMINT GUM. The muscular action of chewing gum will open the eustachian tubes (which lead from the back of the throat to the middle ear.)You can also soothe an earache with OLIVE OIL. Warm and insert a few drops of olive oil into the affected ear, plug with cotton, and apply a hot water bottle.

- Medicines to combat CONSTIPATION AND DIARRHEA are essential. And a heavy duty cold medication. ANTIHISTAMINES, preferably in individually sealed pills, are good for bites, sunburn, and unknown allergies.

- The cruising environment can be conducive to urinary infections. CIPRO works for that, plus aiding diarrhea and seasickness as well.

- Your prescription and routine medicines may go aboard automatically, but consider taking SPARE PRESCRIPTIONS with adequate shelf life. You may be gone longer than you figured. Or use a prescription service. If crossing borders, store pills in their original bottles. Officials get nervous at a mixture of unlabeled ones in plastic bags.

- One of my Sea Sisters depends on Vitamin B6 for PMS.

- A HEATING PAD helps aches and pains, besides keeping you warm.

- EYEGLASSES are important. Besides quality POLARIZED SUNGLASSES, don't forget the straps to keep them from falling overboard. (One of our friends lost the better part of a hundred dollar bill having the diver go after his. He was lucky. It was shallow water.)

- Bring some spare contacts or prescription glasses, and perhaps an old pair with bows removed. They fit inside swim masks, creating an inexpensive prescription mask.

- An easy item to forget is a spare battery(ies) for your hearing aid but, if it's needed, everyone on board will be grateful for your good memory.

- Take lots of peroxide and alcohol. A Sea Sister wrote, "In case of emergency, one tends to pour, not dribble. When my tall husband bashed his head open on an overhead, I fiercely poured on Merthiolate®

at the same moment he instructed, "Squeeze the bottle lightly." Too late. His white hair was pink for days, giving him an over-aged punk rocker look."

- Sanitary napkins not only serve the normal purpose (when female guests are unprepared), but individually wrapped, thus sterile, make wonderful dressings for wounds. (See how long your 12-year-old son will keep one on, however.) They also successfully stuff leaks.

The PRACTICA catalog offers several items that may be of interest. For example:

- A curling iron powered by a flameless, butane energy cell. It's completely safe to store and use anywhere. Effective curling temperature is attained in only 90 seconds, and it has a stay-cool tip and heat-resistant cover. Each replaceable energy cell lasts up to 4½ hours. Curling iron costs $29.95. Replacement energy cells (package of 2) - $7.95.

- Light for anywhere you need it. Great for closets, engine rooms, etc. Simply tap the domed face and softly illuminate any area; tap it again to turn it off. No wiring or outlet needed. Uses 4AA batteries. $14.95

- A comfortable, nifty handle to make carrying grocery bags easier. The wide-gripped handle holds up to 30 lbs. No more ridges in your hands! Set of 2 – $6.95.

All items in the Practica catalog are guaranteed FOREVER. Contact Practica at 1-800-863-5613, or by mail at 89 Tom Harvey Road, Westerly, RI 02891-0999.

JEWELRY

- Our necklaces, bracelets, rings, and earrings tarnish because of *non-use*. Keep them gleaming by placing one or two items in a Ziploc® bag, squeezing out all the air and sealing them.

- And if some pieces have tarnished, there is no need to purchase special "jewelry cleaner." Simply dilute some Top Job cleaner with distilled water and use a toothbrush to clean off the tarnish.

41

PERSONAL STORAGE

- For storage of feminine sanitary products, double bag in Ziplocs® (be sure to squeeze the air out before sealing).

- For disposal of same (or for those who do not put toilet paper through the heads) one Sea Sister suggests the Diaper Genie® available at baby products supply places and even Toys R Us. It works on the basis of a container with a long plastic bag. As you pull the bag from the container, you stuff the material to be disposed of into the end of the bag, twist, and push, sealing it in. No smell, and it takes up no more space than a waste basket. At the end of the cruise, pull out, tie off, and dump in the trash can.

- To store tampons, use a plastic, airtight jar with a screw lid. (Sam's or CostCo's 40-ounce size of Jif peanut butter jars are perfect for this.)

SAFETY TIPS

Usually it is no fun to think about preventive safety. After all, that forces you to consider all the BAD things you're hoping to avoid. Denial, while convenient, is impractical, foolish, and risky.

Think of safety as *seamanship*. It has a much better ring, and oftentimes a change in perspective can prompt positive action. It's a change for the better. Besides, it IS good seamanship to be conscious and concerned about the safety and security of both the boat and the crew.

Make sure that everyone on board knows the location of PFDs, fire extinguishers, and radio. As you travel, you might want to gradually add information about anchoring, signaling devices, or whatever seems pertinent to your boating situation. Be certain that everyone knows where the First Aid kit and book are located.

80% of drowning victims were not wearing PFDs. Evidently some people do not heed the reminder that *PFDs can't work if they're not worn.*

- Find a vest that is comfortable enough so that you'll WEAR IT. Learn which type is most reliable for the job you might demand of it. Buy one that's adequate for the kind of boating you do.

- On a calm day, have the whole crew don their PFDs and go for a swim so that everyone gets used to the feel of her "device." This is particularly recommended if children are aboard, but certainly everyone will benefit from such an exercise. Then try the same drill on a breezy day, in controlled circumstances: one by one, attached to a tether with a dinghy nearby.

- PRACTICE with safety harnesses so that you're comfortable using them.

- NEVER LEAVE THE COCKPIT or steering station without telling another person where you're going.

- PRACTICE CREW-OVERBOARD PROCEDURES so that you know what to do before an accident happens.

- Attach a whistle to each PFD.

- Put STRIPS OF REFLECTIVE TAPE on foul-weather jackets, PFDs, and safety harnesses so that a search light will be more likely to spot you.

- PERSONAL STROBES should be permanent attachments to PFDs. The brighter, the better. Be sure to check batteries regularly.

- Plan, and know ahead of time how you would RESCUE A PET that goes overboard.

FIRE EXTINGUISHERS

The U. S. Coast Guard requires a certain number and type of fire extinguishers, depending on the size of the vessel. But remember, these are *minimums* only. Keep a fire extinguisher anywhere you might use one.

43

Whenever you need one, you'll need it *quickly*, so the more accessible they are, the better.

- Have your fire extinguishers checked and recharged each year.

- Each crew member should practice using the fire extinguisher at least once.

- Directing the extinguisher to the *base* of the fire with a back-and-forth sweeping motion is the most effective way to use a fire extinguisher. The discharge time of small extinguishers is less than a minute.

MORE IDEAS FOR GOOD SEAMANSHIP

- Include a SPOTLIGHT (preferably portable and easily connected) and/or a good, working flashlight to your list of safety items so that you'll be able to spot reflective tape on PFDs, in addition to unlighted markers at night, or scan a riverbank or shoreline.

- Learn the basic rules of the road. And make sure that anyone you put at the helm knows them, too.

- Post in conspicuous areas:
    - Basic Rules of the Road
    - Crew-overboard procedures
    - CPR instructions

These are important if there are children on board, but also for guests, too. Don't assume that everyone is familiar with these aspects of boating. Practice safe boating. Courses are plentiful:

The American Red Cross, www.redcross.org

BOAT/U.S., 800-336-2628, www.boatus.com

U. S. Coast Guard Auxiliary – See the government pages of your phone book

USCG's Boater Safety Hotline, 800-368-5647

U. S. Power Squadrons. Call toll free 1-888-FOR-USPS, www.usps.org

Also, the Nautical Know How course, approved by the National Association of State Boating Law Administrators and the USCG, is accessible via the Internet at < http://tcmail.com/nauticalknowhow> *Play it safe!*

MORE SAFETY TIPS FROM WOMEN ABOARD

- Once you've bought the package of emergency wood plugs, don't just stow them "somewhere." Through-hull fittings can disappear with a lightning strike, and even the most substantial-looking metal can gradually or suddenly deteriorate because of electrolysis. *Keep a plug next to every through-hull*, tied to it because that's the only way to make sure it stays put.

- Establish an "abandon-boat plan". Make a list of what goes with you and what to pack it in. Once you've made the list, post it where it can be found easily and hope you never have to read it again.

- Don't get in too much of a hurry or try to cover too much ground in a limited time span, and don't allow schedules to override your good sense when the weather is bad! Going because you just 'have to get there' to meet someone's schedule, when your gut feeling tells you that you shouldn't, is a good way to get yourself and your boat knocked around. Try to plan ahead for weather delays, and keep yourselves (*especially guests)* prepared with alternate, backup plans.

- Whenever we attached a shore water hose to our boat, we worried about one of the interior water lines breaking aboard the boat, *allowing an unlimited amount of water* into the bilge. Sinking at the dock is among a boater's most embarrassing nightmares! An inexpensive solution is to attach a sprinkler timer (the kind that has a dial to indicate the number of gallons you want—it goes up to 1200 gallons or so.) We put this sprinkler timer on the dock faucet and then attached our water hose to it. We dial it to between 800 and 1200 gallons and reset it every 1-3 weeks. That way, if a water hose on the boat should ever break, only that amount of water would come into the boat, and the bilge pump would be able to keep up before giving out. It's a happy compromise between turning off our shore water faucet every day, and not having any protection at all.

- Check to be sure your hatches CAN be opened from the inside in the event of an emergency! If your hatch covers snap to the deck instead of the hatch itself, chances are that you won't be able to. Having snaps added to the hatch cover itself is a inexpensive correction. One member learned this while watching a boat fire at 3:30 a.m. one morning. A fire on board nearly cost the owners sleeping aboard their lives!

- **Never spend more than 30 seconds fighting a fire. If the fire can't be extinguished, get everyone off the boat.**

TIPS REGARDING MOTION SICKNESS

- Try candied ginger as an alternative to commercial motion-sickness drugs. It has no adverse effects like dry mouth, drowsiness, or blurry vision.

- Do not travel on an empty stomach— have a light, bland meal about an hour before leaving.

- Don't drink alcoholic beverages just before or during the trip.

- Sit in the most stable parts of the boat, keep your head steady, and concentrate on looking at the horizon.

- Try a *sip* of Creme de Menthe for seasickness.

- Emetrol works for vomiting.

- Ask your doctor about Promethazine. It will make you sleepy, but the queasiness will be gone.

- Valium helps to calm your stomach from rolling seas or just plain fear.

- Sea bands are popular.

- Try soda crackers or ginger to ease the churning stomach. A delicious way to eat the latter in in ginger jellies (recipe follows). A Dutch respondent recommends sour apples. A Canadian sailing instructor says the Relief Band does the job. It is a specialized TENS machine, and gives instant relief without drugs or side effects. More expensive though.

GINGER JELLIES

2 - 1 oz. packages gelatin
4-1/3 cups sugar
8 oz. fresh ginger, peeled, chopped coarsely
Powdered sugar

Coat an 8" square pan with vegetable oil cooking spray. Set aside. Put 2 cups water in large sauce pan. Sprinkle gelatin over surface and let soften about four minutes. Add sugar. Warm slowly over low heat, stirring with a wooden spoon until sugar dissolves (about 10 minutes). Increase heat and bring to boil. Add ginger. Reduce heat to medium-low and boil steadily for 15 minutes. Watch carefully to prevent boiling over. Reduce heat if necessary.

Let stand 10 minutes, then pour through a strainer into prepared pan. Allow to sit, uncovered, for 24 hours. Then cut ginger jellies into 1" squares and roll lightly in powdered sugar. Sugared jellies will keep in a plastic container, tightly sealed and refrigerated, for about two months.

GINGER BEER

NOTE: Try to make it ahead of any possibly rough cruises and start drinking it the night before you leave (or head into it). I think it tastes much better and is certainly easier to store than the (glass) bottled ones you can buy at marine stores for a couple of dollars a bottle.

You'll need one jar or bottle larger than 32 oz. (I use the Rubbermaid plastic "bottles" with measurement markers on the side because they don't leak.)

Ingredients:

One large piece of ginger root (this would be about 1+ oz., peeled and crushed). It lasts a long time. I have not yet tried to make it from dehydrated ginger root, but it should work as well.

1/3 cup lime juice
Peel of 3 small limes or 1 lemon
1/2 cup sugar
3-3/4 cups boiling water
1/4 tsp. yeast
1/4 cup lukewarm water

Combined the crushed ginger, lime peel, juice and sugar in the bottle. Pour in the boiling water. Cover loosely and let cool at room (boat) temperature.

Dissolve the yeast in the lukewarm water and add to mixture in bottle. Seal the bottle as tightly as possible and let stand at room temperature overnight. Chill, if possible, strain, and serve! If you have refrigeration, this will last weeks.

DITCH BAG CONTENTS
(Or, what one takes in case they need to leave the boat quickly in an emergency situation)

Following are the contents of Bob and Nela Wilems', *Wave Dancer*, Ditch Bag. Please modify for your own personal needs:

EPIRB
Life Vests—with whistle and light

Vinegar, 2 - 16 oz. jars
Hydrogen Peroxide—1 small bottle
Meat Tenderizer—1 small jar
30 vitamin tablets
Dry Skin Lotion—1 small jar
Eye Drops—1 small bottle
Ibuprofen—2 small jars (50 tablets each)
Silvadene Cream (antibacterial prescription)—1 tube
Vaseline—1 pocket-size tube
"Carmex"—1 small jar

Ace Bandage—1 small
Sunscreen (SPF 30)
Aloe Vera Gel (4 oz.)

Salt Tablets
Pepto-Bismol (4 oz.)
20 Band-Aids
20 butterfly closures or steri-strips
Neosporin (1 oz.)
Surgical Gloves, 6
Eye Pad, 1
Adhesive Pads (12 various sizes)
Surgical Sutures, 6
Surgical Tape—1 small roll
Gauze—2 small rolls
Sea-sickness tablets (i.e. Bonine)
Wash cloth for personal hygiene (1 per person)
1 Dial anti-bacterial liquid soap
1 bar of soap (hotel size—*Zest* suds in salt water)
Toilet Paper, 1 roll
Moist Towelettes
1 Comb

Vienna Sausages, 4 small cans
Pudding, 4 small cans
Selected self-opening cans of food
Selected freeze-dried food
Hard candy
Jar of salt
5x7 spiral notebook
2 pencils
2 pens
1 indelible marking pen to leave notes on whatever if needed

Plastic wrap (1 small box—to make a water still, etc.)
Small plastic cutting board
2 sheathed filet knives
1 gaff (cork pointed end)
Filet instructions
1 wash cloth (to wipe off and dry fish)
Ziploc bags (10 snack, 2 gallon, 4 quart, 4 pint size)
Plastic bailer

Large sponge
Cotton socks (2 pair per person)
Cotton gloves (1 pair per person)
2 space blankets
1 pair of garden gloves for handling fish, etc.
Sunglasses (1 pair per person)
1 whistle
2 small waterproof flashlights
1 hand-bearing compass
2 miniature toothbrushes and 2 small tubes of toothpaste
3 Bic lighters
4 boxes of matches
Embroidery scissors, 1 pair
1 small mirror for signaling
2 collapsible cups
2 small packages of tissues
1 coil (30 ft.) tooth-proof fishing wire (86# test)
18 fishing hooks (sizes 4, 2, and 1/0)
2 packages of 100 yds. 17# test fishing line
1 pair large hemostats
1 pair small pliers
1 small Phillips-head screwdriver
Hand-held flares (3)
Flare gun set (also have all other flares on your boat handy so you can get them on the raft—if there's time!)

NOTES

Buy miniatures and small sizes (a couple of miniatures is better than one large in case of loss or contamination).
Bag *everything* in Ziploc bags.

CHILDREN, BOATS,
AND *WOMEN ABOARD*

BOATING WITH CHILDREN, by Dr. Ethan Welch

I once saw a quote from the writer Robert Benchley that compared traveling with children to "traveling third class by train in Bulgaria." It may not be for everyone, but traveling or boating with children can be a most rewarding and unforgettable adventure for both parents and offspring. From my own experience (we have four children), I can say that our boating and traveling experiences are cherished memories, frequently embellished in the telling and retelling of stories. There are a number of common sense recommendations for recreational boating and travel.

Planning is a must. Parents should keep in mind the goals of the travel. Plans should include the children's input. Allow rest stops along the way, particularly for travel to and from boating grounds. As a parent, you may not mind having a few parts of the travel planned on a "play it by ear" basis, but this may be difficult for children. Book and secure reservations to allow as few failures as possible. When possible, ask for bulkhead seats for maximum room on airlines. In addition to your own requirements lists, generate a list for each of the children several weeks ahead of the trip. The exercise gets everyone thinking and planning; anticipation is part of the fun.

For extended voyages or overseas travel, a visit or phone call to your pediatrician is advisable. Immunizations should not be given at the last moment. If anyone in the group is on medication, be sure to secure enough for the trip. Check appropriate dosage for pediatric requirements, particularly for a general broad-spectrum antibiotic. Carrying a portable cooler for beverages is always a good idea, whether during flying or aboard a vessel. Paying attention to hydration in the young traveler is important. Avoid salty junk food and caffeinated drinks.

One common question regarding traveling with young children is, "How young is too young?" Should a nursing mother plan on that charter vacation? I think much depends on the mother's tolerance to the boating experience, or to travel in general. There is no doubt that breast feeding certainly is convenient, but if the mother gets seasick, then somebody has two very big problems to solve. Again, common sense is the answer. For the older infant, extra baby food and dehydrated food is an answer to travel needs.

So age itself is not a final restriction, but knowing how to keep youngsters safe on a boating trip and aware of the dangers of the water is a full-time job. My suggestion is to start young, but not too young. The comfort level is yours to decide.

I recommend carrying the first aid kit as part of carry-on baggage. It is amazing how many times you need a Band-Aid while going or coming from your destination. Medications may be checked by your pediatrician, but should include the following:

1 Decongestants
2 Throat lozenges
3 Anti-diarrhea medications
4 Pain and fever relievers, such as aspirin or Tylenol
5 Anti-nauseants for motion sickness
6 Topical ointments such as hydrocortisone (1%)
7 General items such as sunscreen, insect repellent, thermometer, and lip balm

For tropical destinations, mosquito netting is an essential item. The supplies and medications for your young travelers should complement your regular adult first aid kit. Carrying an extra pair of glasses and sunglasses for everyone in the carry-on luggage is a good idea, particularly in the event of lost baggage.

The phone list should include, in addition to your pediatrician, emergency phone numbers and poison control center numbers.

If your plans include travel to unusually remote destinations, contact the International Association for Medical Assistance to Travelers (IAMAT) for a list of English-speaking physicians in the area. IAMAT is located at 417 Center Street, Lewiston, NY 14092. Other emergency numbers include the International SOS Association at 800-523-8930.

For each destination, put together a list of points of interest along the way that will enrich the experience. Spend some time with your travel agent on this aspect. If planning to snorkel while sailing in the Caribbean, for example, do a little research on the sea life that you anticipate identifying. We found keeping a log of the travel experience a marvelous help in recalling various adventures. For the older child, learning to keep a journal or sketchbook is fun and can become a lifetime habit.

Above all, don't forget the big picture. Everyone wants to HAVE FUN. Leave some unscheduled time to be creative. Spending leisure time together can give families a marvelous opportunity to communicate, often about topics they might not find comfortable talking about at home. Traveling together is a grand time to get to know everyone better by just having fun. And who knows? Even Bulgaria by train may not turn out to be all bad.

Dr. Ethan Welch, is the founder of MEDICAL SEA PAK CO. He is Emeritus Clinical Professor of surgery at the University of Rochester School of Medicine and Dentistry. He received an AB from Harvard University and MD degree from Johns Hopkins University.

HOMESCHOOLING CHILDREN ABOARD

Long before we had children, we suspected that kids who grew up on boats were the best children in the world in terms of their behavior, education, and appreciation of their environment. It was when we lived aboard the first time, in the Keys back in the '70's, where we encountered several cruising families. It always seemed that these kids were the first ones on the dock to help a new boat tie up. They seemed so self-assured and independent. They were able to talk to people of all ages, not just those of their own age group, and usually on a more mature level than one might expect.

Now that we've lived aboard for almost seven years with our own kids, we are convinced. Boating families are *together* families. There is no doubt in my mind that our children are very different than their peers. They have grown up in an atmosphere that places a higher value on who a person is rather than what a person has. Peer pressure doesn't exist, and they are becoming the kind of people they want to become.

Raising children aboard is a personal decision, but the point is that living aboard or going on an extended cruise doesn't HAVE to wait until the kids are grown and on their own.

The subject of "where the kids will go to school" always comes up when considering raising children aboard. My husband and I are former teachers and we believe that education in and of itself is a life-long process, not just something that "happens" for 12 or 16 years. If you are thinking about raising children on board, you'd best find out what educational options are available and learn to discuss the matter in a knowledgeable way. Well-meaning grandparents (who are going to worry anyway) will be very concerned about *their* grandchildren's education.

Growing numbers of families are choosing home-teaching as an alternative to regular schooling. In some places, the local school is not the best environment for children, academically, socially, or from the standpoint of basic safety. Thanks to the media, and newspapers in particular, much attention is now being paid to homeschooling. News such as the 1997 National Spelling Bee champion being homeschooled makes headlines.

There are many magazines and books that are recommended for anyone contemplating this educational adventure.

MAGAZINES
Growing Without Schooling, 617-864-3100
<HoltGWS@aol.com>

Home Education Magazine, 800-236-3278
Website: www.home-ed-magazine.com

54

BOOKS

Learning All the Time, by John Holt (ISBN 0-201550911)

Home School: Taking the First Step, by Borg Hendrickson (ISBN 0-945519-08-7)

Homeschooling for Excellence, by David and Micki Colfax (ISBN 0-446-38986-2)

The Art of Education, by Linda Dobson (ISBN 0-945097-26-3)

You CAN Teach Your Child Successfully, by Ruth Beechick (ISBN 0-940319-04-7)

There are many, many more. (This is a hot topic!) Check out your local library or favorite bookstore. Also surf the Internet. There are a LOT of homeschooling websites!

* * *

Many cruising families use CORRESPONDENCE SCHOOLS. There are quite a few to choose from. Some of them are:

Calvert School, 105 Tuscany Rd., Baltimore, MD 21210, phone: 410-243-6030. To grade 8 only. Great reputation. Quite structured.

The **American School** offers a high school program. The program has an excellent reputation. The address is 850 East 58th St., Chicago, IL 60637.

High school correspondence courses offered by **University Extension, University of California - Berkeley**, CA 94720.

University of Nebraska Independent Study High School, Continuing Education Center, Rm. 269, Lincoln, NE 68583.

There are more trustworthy schools. For many more, including those offering college level courses, see *Peterson's Independent Study Catalog,* available in most libraries.

We support a concept known as "interest-initiated, child-led learning" or "unschooling." To understand what it's all about, think about how YOU would have filled your school days if you were free to learn whatever you wanted. You would, most likely, have followed your natural tendency to find out as fully as possible about the things that interested you, whether that be oceanography, photography, art, music, horticulture, mechanics, art, computers, writing, sailing.

Fortunately, there is a school that supports the concept of unschooling as well as traditional homeschooling programs: **Clonlara School Home-Based Education Program** (1289 Jewett St., Ann Arbor, MI 48104, 313-769-4515). In addition to their many services, they offer several challenging classes via the Internet, mentored by teachers all over the world. Most importantly for families like us, they deal with any legal issues (and absorb any headaches) encountered because we homeschool.

To find out more about alternative schools, see the annual *National Directory of Alternative Schools*. Many of the alternative schools listed are friendly and helpful to homeschoolers, and it includes a valuable section on homeschooling with descriptions of support groups all over the country. Order from National Coalition of Alternative Community Schools, 58 Schoolhouse Rd., Summertown, TN 38483.

Also, *The Teenage Liberation Handbook: How to quit school and get a real education,* by Grace Llewellyn (ISBN 0-9629591-0-3) is a great sourcebook for older homeschoolers, as well as being an excellent book on education.

Don't forget that **local boards of education** are *sometimes* sympathic to families who are are cruising for periods of one year or less. Also, some local school systems have their own home-education programs. Call your local school to find out what's available in your area. An excellent website to refer to for legal ramifications regarding homeschooling is www.hslda.org.

* * *

For a number of years, one Sea Sister and her husband cruised British Columbia and Alaska with their sons. It is not uncommon to go days and weeks on end without seeing another boat unless one is buddy boating. This Sea Sister is an avid supporter of buddy boating with at least one other couple with kids if one is cruising with kids in these waters. Since fishing and whale-watching provide just a limited amount of entertainment for youngsters and teenagers, she feels it's best to spend more time at docks when traveling with children. It's a lot easier for them to get off the boat to meet and spend time with other children. Now that she's cruising in Mexico, this Sea Sister often hears people "advertising children aboard" via VHF nets in order to hook-up with other cruisers with children.

TIPS ON CRUISING WITH KIDS

- Get the kids involved! Even grammar school kids can do the math to figure the scope needed to safely set the anchor.

- They can help plan each day's route. Multiply average expected speed by the time available until you would like to be secured for the night in order to find the maximum comfortable distance you can cover in a day. Then check the guides for a suitable marina or anchorage near that location. For short distance cruisers, there are still lots of variables that the kids can consider. The more involved the children are, the more fun they'll have and the more accomplished they'll feel.

- They can learn to steer, read a compass, follow a chart, cleat down a line and throw it. Knot tying and learning to stow lines and fenders properly are basics for children living around the water.

- Do rotate watches. A certain length of time "on-duty" followed by time "off-duty" breaks up the sometimes tedious wait for youngsters anxious to "get there." It also keeps everyone aware of where they are, and how they got there. These skills, and the ability to use the radio, may save lives somewhere down the line. Remember, the most skilled captain may eventually be incapacitated by illness or injury. Your family and even your guests may be the only possible way to get the boat back to shore.

- It's important to get input from the whole family during the planning stages of any adventure. Everyone should be able to have a voice in where they will go and what they will see and do as they travel.

- Keep a supply of books about various aspects of where you are and where you're going so that children —as well as adults—can learn about things that exist beyond the beach border of a state or country.

- Often what begins as "play" evolves into a learning activity, so encourage the natural sequence of events. Children's minds are like sponges: they absorb a lot. Take this natural curiosity and channel it into an awareness of the world around the boat. Soon they won't miss the mall.

- Establish boat rules early, making sure they aren't all "don'ts." To function as a good team, everyone must feel that they are needed. Assign chores and jobs, equally mixing the have-to-do's and the want-to-do's.

- Before a cruising trip, the whole family should go to a local YMCA and/or sports club pool to learn swimming safety and CPR.

- Teach basic piloting and navigation as soon as your child shows interest.

- Allow older children to steer and stand short watches.

- Look at the stars of the night sky. Talk about how mariners of old navigated to uncharted lands. Introduce mythology.

- Books on tape provide an excellent way to pass the time, especially when you're underway, standing watch, or holed up inside the boat due to bad weather.

- Emphasize the importance of privacy and alone-time. It's a good idea to set aside a certain hour of day to spend with one's self, reading, journalizing, writing letters, etc.

- Give each child a "Do Not Disturb" indicator so that the concept of privacy can exist even if the reality is marginal.

- Consider having your child's best friend join you for part of your cruise. Not only can the anticipation of seeing friends be exciting, but it gives your child the chance to show off *her* world.

- Encourage letter writing. When sharing their experiences on an on-going basis, writers are more likely to pay attention to the details of each new discovery.

- The ability to play a musical instrument provides loads of entertainment, both for the musician AND his audience!

- Include state or national parks on your itinerary. When you get there, find a ranger and get a full tour. Their enthusiasm is entertaining and oftentimes contagious!

- If the park isn't staffed, find local information and have your own expedition.

- Have each child keep a combination diary/log/photo album.

- The memories of unique times and special places will last long after the cruise is over.

- For safety's sake, develop some easily recognized ship-to-shore signals for dinghy pick-ups or general attention-getters. Batteries have been known to run out in handheld radios.

- If teenagers are out, especially with the dinghy at night, <u>check-in time is not an approximate</u>—even in home port. The reasons should be obvious. Give each child a handheld radio for his or her 13th birthday and explain that parents don't want to be worriers...it just goes along with the territory.

TIPS ON COMBINING TRAVEL AND LEARNING

ENGLISH - RESEARCH - WRITING

- Your local libraries will have lots of information in the form of travel books and magazines. (The local library will order from other libraries any book they do not have.) Write to states, countries, departments of tourism and/or agencies for information on your destination.
- Writing a daily journal.
- Making and writing to pen pals.
- Reading literature.
- Listen to audio tapes, do crossword puzzles.

SOCIAL STUDIES

- Travel books. (They have wonderful history, geography, and cultural sections.)
- Visit historical sights.

- Museums—National, state, county, city. Some of the most unique are in small towns!
- Topography
- Geography
- Cultures—including different cultures in the United States
- The different ways holidays are celebrated
- Genealogy

SCIENCE

- Study the flora and fauna of any place you visit
- Visit science museums
- Ecology: Where better to learn about the ecology of streams, swamps, bays, oceans, rivers than in them?
- Attend classes presented by park rangers, nature centers, etc.
- Read brochures put out by parks and nature centers. Many of these have excellent information about the habitat, flora and geology of the park.
- Anthropology—evidence of human history and prehistory is all around us.

MATHEMATICS/ECONOMICS

- Estimate expenses for day, week, month
- Compute real expenses for day, week, month
- Estimate fuel usage/expense
- Figure out REAL fuel usage/expense
- Figure out miles/gallon
- Estimate how far a destination is
- Plan meals, budget for and buy groceries
- Handling money
- Credit
- Budgeting

MUSIC/ART

- Photo essay of your trips
- Attend local concerts
- Buy whatever supplies are needed to draw, sculpt, sketch
- Draw a picture journal

60

SOCIAL SKILLS/INDEPENDENT LIVING

- Having the opportunity to meet many different people with many different backgrounds
- Learning to handle yourself in many different situations
- Problem-solving within the family travel unit
- Doing without the television, telephone, and many modern conveniences
- Leaving friends at home—learning to be an integral part of the family unit

PHYSICAL EDUCATION

- Sailing, rowing, hauling anchors; but once on shore, walking, hiking, cycling, backpacking
- Learning local dances
- Learning local sports and games

HOME ECONOMICS

- Cooking
- "Making do" with canned stores vs. going to the grocery store and buying something fresh
- Laundering one's own clothes; learning how to use a laundromat

VOLUNTEER OPPORTUNITIES

- Park rangers
- Docents in museums
- Organizations such as The Nature Conservancy and the National Park Service is happy to have volunteers!

PETS ABOARD

SOLVING DOG PROBLEMS ON BOATS

We really enjoy our combined 180 pounds of dog, and even though there is plenty of room on a boat as big as the 44MT-DC, it was not exactly designed for easy dog access from the water and it doesn't have handy grass patches or telephone poles – only two people heads. This article will describe how we solved these problems with two dogs that love the boat and love to swim. *Four Seasons* is now definitely a dog-friendly vessel!!

When we began boating in the Northern California Delta about 13 years ago, we had a 21-foot runabout, a porta-potti, 5-gallons of water and one German shepherd. We did a lot of dock hopping in those days, but gradually learned where acceptable beaches were and began tying out to trees along shore most of the time. It was usually no more than a few feet from the back of the boat to the shore and the dog could jump off whenever he needed to.

We soon learned, however, that hoisting a 100-lb shepherd back onto the boat was something we didn't want to do 4 or 5 times a day. I prototyped a boarding ladder using a 4-foot hardware store stepladder attached to the stainless steel ladder off the swim platform of the runabout. The stainless steel ladder is vertical, and the stepladder extends out from it at about a 30-degree angle.

This worked well, and we were able to train "Shadow" to swim from the beach and come up the ladder. The advantages were that a wet dog is preferable to a sandy dog on a boat, and we didn't have to get wet loading him in.

The stepladder quickly disintegrated under marine use, of course, and was replaced by a teak ladder of approximately the same size and shape that I made. We moved up from the runabout to a 26-foot cruiser, then to a 30-foot cruiser, and finally to a 44-foot DC Marine Trader. We also increased the canine population from one Shepherd to two. (We have a picture of 5 aboard the 30-foot cruiser, but that's another story.) The original teak boarding ladder I built in 1986 has been installed on each and every boat and is still in service. They use it many, many times per day because they both love to chase the tennis ball, so it's on and off, on and off, etc. Even when we are anchored out in the middle of a slough, the dogs get to play and swim. We no longer need to be tied to a beach.

I don't know if you've noticed, but for every problem you solve on a boat, another one (or two) appear. The boarding ladder neatly gets the dog onto the swim platform, but how does he get from there to the deck of the MT? Those little wimpy steps and a transom that has a negative slope are not dog friendly, to say the least. Once again, I prototyped the solution.

I cut two large plywood steps, following the contour of the transom and swim platform, and attached them to the small teak steps,

which exist on the transom of the DC44. I supported them at the four corners by vertical lengths of white PVC pipe with stainless steel threaded rod through them. The bottom step rests on the swim platform through the PVC legs, and the top step rests on the bottom step. I now have two large steps, securely supported, with only two ¼" bolt holes in each of the small teak transom steps – no holes in the transom or the swim step, and very little additional weight or load on the transom or swim platform. This is not only easy for the dogs to get up and down; it is much easier for us.

The plywood steps won't last long, so I plan to replace them with the same size and shape step in white 1" thick plastic, covered with carpet and trimmed around the edge. The PVC pipe legs will give way to stainless steel.

Even with a dog-boarding ladder, it is still a pain to get the dogs to go to shore and come back early in the morning and late at night. They tend to want to be taken to shore in the dinghy rather than jump off. In addition, there are some places where dogs are not welcome ashore. Angel Island in San Francisco Bay is one of those places. We love Angel Island, and go there a lot, but we always had to kennel the dogs before going out there because there were no "facilities" for them. Donna is a planner and organizer, and is constantly working out solutions to problems we face on the boat. Once thought of, however, it is up to me to implement them.

Would there, could there, be any way to build a "pooh-box" for the dogs on the boat? After much foot-dragging, complaining, compromising, and figuring, I had to admit it was feasible. What we came up with is a shallow box, about 2" deep and 24" wide by 48" long. I installed a drain system underneath it consisting of 5 holes with PVC pipe attached and running to one corner. The box sits on stubby legs about 2" tall to give clearance for the plumbing. The inside of the box is heavily epoxied and fiberglassed, and there are two sides and one back piece made of 3/8" plastic which fold down when not being used. These hinge up and fasten together at the top to form a three-sided enclosure about 22" high. One dog is a male, so this is what he aims for.

We installed the box on the forward deck between the two air hatches on either side and just to the rear of the hatch for the forward cabin. Straps to these three points attach the box so it won't fly around. On the side of the cabin, next to where the AC power cord comes in, the previous owners had installed a phone jack. It turns out that the hole was just the right size for a plastic thru-hull fitting, and I ran a light plastic hose from the pooh-box drain, under the windshield, through the fitting and back to the sink in the forward head where I teed into the drain hose. We pick up and bag solid waste, as we do at home, and simply flush the box out several times a day with the wash down hose on the bow.

To try to teach even old dogs new tricks such as "do your business in the box, please" you start by figuring out the type of reward that motivates your dog. In our case it is food, food, and food in that order. Dogs will usually do what you want, especially for a reward. The problem is <u>explaining</u> to them <u>exactly</u> what it is that you want them to do.

You start associating the act or acts with a word ("hurry up" is often used) and reward them when they accomplish <u>your</u> goal. We have used "hurry up" on both dogs since they were puppies. Our backyard is cement with a 2-foot perimeter of plants and gravel, so our first major training use of The Pooh Box was to place it where the gravel is. It took 20 minutes, guidance on a leash, endless repetitions of "hurry up" and a lot of trips in and out of the box before we got lucky. An immediate treat and we were on our way. *No problem mom, how many dog biscuits do you have? How many times would you like me to perform??*

Then, we moved the contraption onto the bow of the boat and vowed to stay on the boat until we achieved success. My resolve was sorely tested. This time it took six hours in the morning and I began to understand despair. One reflects that all those 6:30 a.m. trips to the beach were not all that necessary if they could wait six hours to figure out what their silly human wanted!! The heavier tasks (I'm trying to be delicate here) came automatically within 12 hours.

I can't take room here to go into this training in detail, but there is a short book on the subject. Forgive me, gentle reader, but it is called <u>(In Seven Days or Less!) You Can Teach Your Dog to Eliminate on Command</u>, by Dr. M.L.Smith. It can be ordered by calling 1-800-682-1897. The book is $7.95, plus $2.50 shipping/handling. It is also available at www.Amazon.com.

It was certainly worth the effort. The freedom we have from having to pull into a dock or find a beach is magnificent. Good luck!!

January 2000 Update – Alas, Shadow is now chasing tennis balls in Doggie Heaven. We now have Cody, but all systems still operate just fine. We spent eight days tied to the buoys in Ayala Cove at Angel Island in San Francisco Bay and the dogs never got off the boat. Heidi is the tennis ball maniac and she had to jump in and chase the tennis ball every day or there was just no living with her. That water is cold! We felt soooooooo bad watching the other boaters row their dogs to a certain beach around the corner several times a day.

We replaced the gravel in the Pooh Box with the rubber squares they sell for decking.

(By Russ and Donna Sherwin. Originally published in the Spring 97 issue of the MTOA Newsletter. Reprinted with permission.)

OTHER PET-LOVING SEA SISTERS WRITE...

We will be living aboard with our two German Shepherds who have boated with us for years. They are trained to use a potty pan on the bow, which is lined with Astro turf.

I trained them to use the pan by first lining the pan for a week or so with a piece of sod I picked up at a nursery. Then I made the switch to Astro turf with grass clippings on top so that it would have the scent of grass. Two weeks later, it was just Astro turf on a large 3' x 3' pan. Both dogs are females, making it easier for them to hit the pan.

* * *

"Bart" is a six-year-old Maltese. Friends that could no longer care for him gave him to us. Our Border collie, "Windy," was gone after 15 years of being the best boat dog ever. Bart had never been on a boat! He immediately mastered the steps to the bridge—he loved being up there with us. Short trips were no problem, but we were planning a long run to Canada from Holland, Michigan! Bart had been our resident boat dog for only four months, but he was so willing and easily trainable.

I prepared a box for him—kind of like a dog litter box. It was stout plastic with handles, about 20 x 15 x 4 inches. I lined it with heavy plastic and cut an Astor-turf doormat to fit and sprinkled some leaves and twigs I had gathered from his dog run on top of it.

We left for Canada, and about six hours later, Bart had to do his duty. I walked him around the deck on his leash and led him to his box. Nothing. One hour later, same routine. But this time, Bart did it! The leaves and twigs were properly re-scented. Bart was praised, hugged and given treats. We had a potty-trained boat dog!

* * *

When we acquired our dog (selected to remain fairly small as an adult) as a tiny puppy we already knew that we intended to cruise. Having watched other dog owners making the obligatory dinghy runs to the beach morning and night, we decided that there had to be a better way. Figuring that, if a puppy could be trained to paper, why not a cat box? We bought a large, shallow Rubbermade container and a green plastic 'fake grass' door mat. Each morning, when we knew that our new puppy needed "to go for a walk," we placed her in the box. She crawled out, we put her back in. Eventually she did her business, and got an appropriate reward. Continued training insured that she knew where she was supposed to "perform." Eventually we added a hole punched in the doormat, with a loop of sturdy small stuff tied through it, the better to hang the doormat over the side of the boat to clean it. We also added a thin layer of kitty litter to absorb the liquid and contain its odor. Nearly 8 years later the system still works well. Yes, we usually have kitty litter tracked around on our fore deck, but it isn't near the mess that dinghying dog and owner to muddy beach twice a day would cause. And, an unexpected advantage, when we have to leave her locked inside the boat (or in the rare hotel room while traveling) the kitty litter box moved to a convenient location makes it clear where she is to relieve herself.

* * *

We moved an 11-year-old dog (a 40 lb. Chow) aboard in February 1997 when we bought our DeFever trawler, *Meander*. This is our first boat, so Willow had no other boating experience.

Willow loves getting off the boat when we are docked. New "sniffs" are what dogs live for.

When we are anchored, Willow has her own grass on which to relieve herself. I put two or three chunks of sod on top of two layers of DriDeck on a side deck. The DriDeck allows the sod to drain—Willow hates soggy grass! To get her to use that area, I collected liquid and solid samples from Willow and "salted" her sod the first time. I don't have to "salt" new sod, which I buy about every three months. She begrudgingly uses it and usually walks all the way around the boat two or three times to see if there is a dock and boats (those mean a walk on shore, to her).

We don't put the dinghy down and take Willow to shore from anchorages. The first few times we anchored out she held it all for over 30 hours. We felt awful about this but other pet owners have told us that situation is harder on owners than the pets themselves.

Animals aboard need their own lifejackets—West Marine or any such boat store carries them. I wrote Willow's name and our phone number on the jacket.

Harnesses, instead of any around-the-neck devices, should be used. I saw a dog nearly choke to death a while back. The dog was tied up on the boat's deck and tried to jump off the boat to "check out" my dog. The dog slipped and was hanging overboard by its neck before I could get there to notify the owner. Scary! It turned out OK but if no one had been around, the dog would have died.

Another reason for using a harness is that if a dog falls overboard, a boat hook could be used to pull the dog back to the boat.

I have a metal kennel (cage), which Willow goes into when we're underway and the seas are rough. She hates to be left in the salon when we're cruising and prefers to be on the fly bridge with us so that's where we put the kennel (tied to a support to keep it from moving).

One vet told me that if a dog seems bored or depressed, then longer walks would help alleviate the problem. When we were first aboard, Willow licked one of her feet until Lick Granulomas occurred. I started walking her longer each time out and the granulomas (and probable cause) went away.

When we are cruising in rough waters, I walk Willow, on a leash, to her boat-grass. Because our side decks are narrow, I don't want to risk her going over the side. And since Willow has to turn around a few times before using the sod, she could easily fall over.

* * *

My husband and I have been full-time live aboards for over two years on our Eagle 40 trawler, *Passage*, in Half Moon Bay, CA, along with our (20-pound) cat, Elvis. Elvis adjusted well to life on the boat and seems to like it better than condo living (so much more to see and do!) Here are some tips for keeping cats aboard:

Elvis wears a harness full time which displays 2 ID tags: one tag with our name, boat slip and phone number, and the other with our cell phone number for when we're cruising away from our home port. The harness makes it easy to pull him out of the water if he goes in (which he has).

Nail a long piece of carpet or other sturdy material to the dock and let it hang into the water. If the cat falls in, he can swim to it and pull himself out with his claws. (I would not keep a declawed cat on a boat).

If the cat falls into salt water, always give him a thorough freshwater rinse afterward.

Elvis has a covered litter box which we keep in the saloon overnight and while we're at work. We had a problem with the clumping clay litter as it "clumped" in his paws when he'd been walking on damp decks or docks. We've switched to the new clumping wheat litter (Swheat Scoop) and it's not been a problem. It clumps, but not in Elvis' paws!

Elvis occasionally gets seasick when we're out on the ocean, usually when we haven't had the boat out for a while. We don't give him any medication beforehand and it passes quickly – he gets sick, then goes to sleep and is fine for the rest of the day. If we cruise on successive days, he gets his "sea paws" and has no problem. He prefers to get into his pet taxi while we're underway, as it appears to make him feel more secure.

If the cat is sleeping while underway, don't disturb him by petting, lifting or attempting to move him. We've found that doing so disrupts Elvis's equilibrium and causes him to get sick again.

NEVER leave a cat unsupervised outside the boat. Curious cats will find trouble by getting onto other boats, ingesting toxic substances or falling in the water.

Elvis has no problems with fleas since he lives on the water!

Happy boating with your furry crewmates!

* * *

We currently live aboard our Catalina 36 on an inland lake. By the time you read this, we will have relocated from an inland lake to Dataw Island, off the coast of South Carolina. It is a small island near Fripp Island and Hilton Head and is accessible by bridge. We are full-time live aboards.

We have two Westies (Westhighland Terriers) who are sisters, ages 7½ and 6. The have both been onboard since 6 weeks of age and are seasoned sailors.

They LOVE to swim and our vet has proclaimed them "the most muscular Westies around." They wear their life vests without complaint anytime the boat is in motion. We trained the oldest to the bow, but since the purchase of the second dog and a dinghy, they both look "longingly at shore", and so are spoiled. Hope to remind them of bow duty with the move to the coast.

We do have them trained to float along with us on their float and jump off, swim around, then jump back on. We keep them exercised in the water by making them swim to us or swim to the boat as to keep their muscles up to par just in case they do go overboard. They are hardy little friends and greatly enjoy the boat.

* * *

I am the mother of two liveaboard cats, Buddy and Squeaks. Both cats have been apartment cats since birth and are not allowed outside at all, so I worried about Buddy's adapting to the liveaboard life: he's 13 years old, cranky and timid by nature. Indeed, he has an unfortunate habit of taking drastic revenge if he is upset, usually on my pillow.

Squeaks is younger, easy-going and of a cheerful disposition, so I didn't worry about her at all. In fact, I ended up getting a power boat because Buddy misbehaved so badly on a test sail aboard a friend's sloop—we won't be invited back. He definitely doesn't like boats that heel.

He doesn't like boats that have engines, either. Knowing his wicked ways, I've been covering my bunk with plastic sheeting to head off any revenge he might contemplate. Every time I take *Puffin* out for a cruise, Buddy retreats to the top of the linen locker where he trembles and rolls his eyes in terror until safely back at the dock. I've been taking him for daily short runs in hopes of acclimatizing him, but it's been over a month, and still no signs of easing up.

Squeaks has adapted beautifully. Frightened at first, she now emerges from her hidey-hole under the bunk after the first minutes and even comes up into the cockpit (which is cat-proofed with screening). Like all cats, she likes to sit

71

in the middle of whatever you're doing, so I've set up a box for her in front of the wheel so I can pat her while steering. She eyes the sea birds from her new perch with great interest.

Recently, Buddy has been peeing in his water dish to indicate his displeasure. However, this turns out to be a boon for me. I simply put down another water dish for drinking, and leave the old one (a large plastic dish pan) empty and available for his head. He now uses that in favor of the litter box, saving me a good deal of money and mess. I only wish that Squeaks would follow suit!

Poor old fella, I feel badly about the upset he feels. So badly, in fact, I've decided to move ashore for the winter rather than heading south as I'd originally planned. Furry little tyrant! But I couldn't live without my two dear ones, so that's just the way it has to be.

* * *

What to do about litter that is tracked out of the box? A Dustbuster! We installed a hood-type litter box in the space under our combo washer/dryer. Then, outside the entrance to the box, I put a step, just a three-sided "riser" for them that I covered with Scoot Guard. Indoor/outdoor carpeting would probably work too. Anyway, it helped to catch the litter upon exit. We later added the refinement of a canvas "curtain" with a flap door for them to get in to keep the box out of sight.

A cat (or dog) really makes a boat a home, and I think that we encountered more people WITH pets aboard than those without. I'll get all my experiences together and get back to you.

SOMETIMES THE DOG PADDLE JUST ISN'T GOOD ENOUGH!
By Michael Birkenblit, D.V.M.

When we think of summer we immediately think of fleas and heartworm, possibly even the dangers of heatstroke -but how often do we give adequate thought to drowning? Many pet owners take their pets on boat trips with minimal or no precautions for their safety.

Equally important is some common sense prevention and training.

The "doggy flotation devices" do work, and provide extra flotation for the exhausted dog that does not know how to "float" and conserve his strength pending rescue. They should be considered as necessary for a pet under way that is far from shore or in rough weather as a life jacket for a small child under similar circumstances.

Can you physically lift your soaking wet and probably struggling dog onto your boat from the water? The freeboard (distance from the water to the deck or top edge of your boat) is frequently so great that this is impossible, especially on sailboats. Practice this "dog overboard" drill while on your mooring; if you cannot manage it under these ideal conditions, you certainly will not be able to manage in an emergency.

Ensure that your dog can swim well enough that he won't panic; don't believe the old saying "all dogs can swim" will hold true if your pet is suddenly thrown overboard in choppy water. A terrified, thrashing dog will be exhausted in minutes, and it will take more than minutes to get turned around and maneuver close enough to help him. If you have a water-loving dog, ensure that his training is such that he will not dive in without permission.

Invent and practice a game getting Rover to swim to a life-ring—a small sound-producing device. A small dog can perch on and cling to a life ring; a larger dog can easily hold on with his front legs. A dog that will swim to (and into) a life ring lowered from a boat can be pulled aboard even a boat with high freeboard. If you have a swim platform or ladder, teach the dog to swim around the boat and use it! This is also a "must" for the home with a swimming pool: TRAIN your dog until he can locate easily and use steps and ladders and can confidently exit on his own.

If your vessel is large enough that the dog may not be in your sight at all times, consider confining the dog to a safe area, or using a bell or other sound-producing device to keep your aware of his whereabouts.

Ensure that your pet has identification tags just in case he becomes dependent on the kindness of strangers. If you do a lot of boating, consider a special boat collar and tag with the name of your vessel, homeport, and radio call sign, as well as your name, address and telephone number.

Obvious safety rules should be observed for pets as well as people; don't allow your dog to "bow ride." He'll love standing in the bow of your power boat with the wind streaming through his ears; he'll also get a bad wind and salt burn in his eyes, and if he loses his balance he'll go right through your propellers before you can react.

Provide sunscreen for your shorthaired, light-skinned dog, or for your dark-coated critter that must come off the water and into the show ring. The combination of sun and wind causes dehydration far more quickly than ashore; provide cool water or ice frequently.

Keep his nails short so he doesn't skid across the decks (he can't grab a stanchion like you do!), and ensure that fishing equipment is properly stowed so he doesn't get "fish-hooked." Boating is fun for beast as well as man-even our cat has gone along on a cruise! Accidents can happen quickly, however, and help is not always close enough at hand to prevent a tragedy. A bit of foresight and a few minutes of training may well save your dog's life, and save you a lifetime of guilt.

A FIRST AID KIT FOR YOUR PET

Although many of your own first aid items are suitable for dogs, it is preferable to keep a separate kit. Dealing with a pet at the site of an accident or with signs of a serious illness is a job for the vet. You can decide if you are capable of helping your pet with a minor problem or you can elect to call the vet. Initially, giving first aid may be your only option to help your pet until you can reach a vet or hospital, especially if you are anchored at a remote site when the problem occurs. Many accidents are minor, requiring only the safe application of basic first aid and common sense.

1. Round-ended scissors (or bandage scissors found at medical supply store)

2. Rectal thermometer: lubricate and insert 1 inch into the anus and wait two minutes before removing to read (normal temp is 100.4-102.2 degrees F)

3. Tweezers: used for removal of ticks from the skin or debris from a minor wound

4. 2 inch and 4 inch bandages (rolls)

5. 2 inch adhesive tape dressing (rolls)

6. Lint gauze (various sizes)

7. Sterile cotton and large rolls of cotton

8. Old socks: used for covering bandages and discouraging pet from licking

74

paw wound or to cover front paws when pet is pawing its eyes when eye irritation is present

9. Plastic bags: used for keeping foot dressings dry

10. Antiseptic cream, Neosporin or Pantalog (from your vet): used topically only, apply to abraded, irritated or broken skin

11. Antiseptic wash such as Chlorhexi Derm Flush/topical antiseptic (from your vet): washing minor wounds or irritated, localized reddened area of skin

12. Q tips

13. Kaolin or kaopectate: used with minor enteritis causing a diarrhea stool (1 tsp., 3x/day for small dogs; 1 dessert spoon, 3x/day for large. The dosage depends on the body weight of the animal and a vet can provide an answer for a safe dosage)*

14. Calamine lotion: used for localized reddened area from a flea bite or dermatitis

15. Eye irrigating solution (from your vet): used for rinsing a foreign body or discharge from the eye

16. Ear cleaner such as Otic Clear (from your vet): used to clean the ear canal, especially following swimming/normal bathing to prevent build-up of wax or infections from bacteria

17. Soft material muzzle or you can make one from a bandage: used when a dog has been injured or appears to be in acute pain * *

* Ask your vet what dietary regimen can be followed to stop simple vomiting and diarrhea (associated with mild gastritis or enteritis). Remember vomiting and diarrhea can be signs of poison ingestion or serious illness. Contact the vet immediately if you are suspicious in any way or if the symptoms persist after dietary adjustment.

**A frightened dog in pain may try to bite, so a muzzle or an improvised muzzle is a sensible precaution. Once applied, watch the dog closely for troubled breathing. If troubled breathing begins to develop, remove the muzzle immediately. You can open the pet's mouth, pull the tongue forward and then reapply the muzzle, keeping it loose and then hold the dog's head in your lap.

• Never muzzle a dog with suspected chest injuries or if they are having difficulty breathing before applying the muzzle.

- Never leave a muzzled dog alone.

- Never muzzle a short nose breed, you may impair its breathing.

TIPS FOR HAVING PETS ABOARD

- Keep cats from tracking litter by placing a mat made of grass or artificial turf in front of the litter box. The rough surface of the mat will remove pieces of litter from the cat's paws when it climbs out of the box.

- Fido and Fleas: Fleas are a nuisance, especially in the temperate south where they abound all year round. Try adding a little vinegar to Fido's drinking water (not so much that he won't drink it). This discourages the little varmints and your pup will be much more comfortable. Much less expensive than the commercial anti flea preparations.

- Another suggestion from observation. Seems one sailor with a large (nearly 100 pound) dog told her that he used a fireplace log carrier to lift their dog when the distance from dinghy to boat was too far for the dog to jump. He was pleased with the discovery because the carrier supported the dog securely and required only one hand (leaving one hand free for the owner to hang on to something for his <u>own</u> safety)!

- When hot weather settles in, don't forget to take care of your four-legged boating companions. Besides checking that they always have water available, put a few reusable POLAR PACKS in the freezer for them. Slip one in a Ziploc bag and let them lie on it to help keep them cool.

- Don't forget heartworm medication for both dogs and cats.

- Also, consider having your dog vaccinated against Lyme disease. It's far cheaper and gentler on your pet than treating the life-long symptoms.

- Remember to take your pet's paperwork! A health certificate signed by a veterinarian is usually required to take a pet ashore in some countries. Remember, though, that other countries may not allow them entry at all, regardless of paperwork. <u>The health certificate must be less than 30 days old to enter Canada.</u>

- If necessary, pet's medications.

76

- Ask your vet for a printout of your pet's health records. If your pet gets ill while you are traveling, the new vet will have a professional background report from which to start diagnosis.

- "Traveling with Your Pet" is a booklet listing regulations for interstate and international travel: Write: ASPCA Education Department, 424 East 92nd Street, New York, NY 10128

TIPS FOR CRUISING WITH YOUR PET
INTO THE COMMONWEALTH OF THE BAHAMAS

Important US/Florida Phone Numbers

- USDA: U.S. Department of Agriculture/Gainesville Office: 1-800-342-0395. For questions regarding the various domestic animal import requirements when planning a cruise with your pet(s) outside of the continental United States.

- USDA/Miami Office: 305-526-2926. This office is open Monday through Friday and is located near the airport.

- US Public Health Service/Miami office: 305-526-2910

Commonwealth of the Bahamas Import Requirement

- An import permit application is required for each <u>species</u> of domestic animals (pets) that you plan to have cruising with you to the Bahamas. Two dogs require only one pet import permit application; a dog and a cat would require two separate pet import permit applications.

- The application is obtained from the Ministry of Agriculture, Trade and Industry (in Nassau) or the Bahamas Consulate (in Miami). It must be completed by you and then forwarded, via either priority mail or regular mail, to the USDA office for endorsement. After endorsement, it will be returned to you by mail.

77

- I suggest that you make a copy of the endorsed application and have it with you when you arrive in the Bahamas. You must send a $10.00 money order, the processing fee for one application. It should be made payable to the Director of Agriculture, Ministry of Agriculture with the original USDA endorsed pet import application to the following address:

> Director of Agriculture
> Department of Agriculture
> P. O. Box N-3028
> Nassau, Bahamas

> Telephone number: 242-325-7502 or 325-7509
> Fax: 242-325-1767

- Your pet MUST be 6 months of age or older to gain entry into the Bahamas.

- You MUST have a valid certificate proving the pet has been vaccinated against rabies not less than 1 month or more than 10 months prior to importation of the pet into the Bahamas.

- You MUST possess an International Veterinary Health Certificate (acquired from your licensed veterinarian) for the pet, which is presented within 48 hours of arrival into the Commonwealth of the Bahamas.

Additional Suggestions

- Make certain you start the permit process about 4 weeks prior to your planned Bahamas cruise to insure you meet each requirement by your cruising date. The permit is valid for 90 days from the date of issuance. The Bahamas government is not concerned with when your pet leaves the Bahamas but the listed requirements must be met in order to gain entry for your pet when you arrive and clear customs.

If you have any questions about securing a pet's import permit application beyond this explanation, you can contact the Bahamas Consulate in Miami, at 305-373-6295 (after 9:30 a.m.) Your questions will be answered and a copy of the import permit application can be mailed to you direct or faxed at your request from the Consulate's office.

In the Galleys of WOMEN ABOARD

KEEPING FRUIT AND VEGETABLES FRESH

Keeping fresh fruit and vegetables on long cruises can be a problem because a grocery store isn't always "just around the corner." Here are some tips on proper storage of produce.

- Carefully select firm, nearly ripe produce and take the time to store it properly to insure its freshness for a maximum length of time.

- When you bring fresh fruits and vegetables aboard, wash them in a sink of soapy water with about a 1/4 cup of bleach for about a minute to keep them from mildewing.

- *Rinse them thoroughly* (especially all citrus fruit, apples, potatoes, melons, tomatoes, and cucumbers.) Citrus fruits have been known to last up to 4 weeks without refrigeration after such preparation. Potatoes last even longer without growing new 'plants' from their eyes.

- *Dry everything thoroughly!* Place vegetables in "Ziploc® Vented Vegetable Bags" (green box) before storing in refrigerator.

- Citrus fruits, onions, and potatoes may be hung in orange (open air) citrus bags rather than refrigerating. To keep hanging fruit from bruising while on a port or starboard tack, bungee them in to reduce the swinging action.

- Onions should not be washed—they do not do well after washing because it is impossible to completely dry them.

- Tomatoes, cucumbers, squash, zucchini, kiwi fruit, carrots, and green peppers may be washed in the same way to enhance storage time, but require refrigeration. Refrigerate these items in vented Ziploc® bags with a dry paper towel to absorb any residual liquid.

- All fruits and vegetables: If kept in a tightly closed plastic bag, fruits and vegetables will use up all the available oxygen and expel carbon dioxide. They will "suffocate" and lose color, flavor, texture and nutrients.

- Place several paper towels on the bottom of the vegetable drawer of your refrigerator. They will absorb excess moisture. Even better: a plastic doily (if you can find one) will help air to circulate.

- Bananas: If they are too green to eat, store them in a paper bag with apples, which give off the ethylene gas that accelerates ripening.

- Onions and potatoes: Do NOT store them together. Onions give off gases that alter the flavor of the potatoes, and the potatoes' moisture makes the onions sprout.

- If you buy potatoes by the bag, add an apple to the bag for storage. Apples give off ethylene gas, which helps prevent sprouting.

- Citrus fruits, such as oranges, lemons, limes and grapefruit can be stored in string bags in a cool place. If the lemons or limes should turn hard and dry, they can be freshened for use by soaking overnight in lukewarm water or by being placed in boiling water for five minutes.

- Store fresh mushrooms in a paper bag to prevent dampness, which causes them to turn brown.

- A completely dry storage is best for lettuce. If possible, buy it before the outer leaves have been removed. Don't trim off these leaves, but let them dry up instead. When ready to use, peel them off and a good solid head of lettuce will be underneath. For this method of lettuce storage, it is essential that air be allowed to circulate around the entire head. Place the lettuce in string bags or wire mesh baskets and hang them away from direct sunlight; the heads can be kept five weeks or more.

- Green peppers should be wrapped tightly in waxed paper. Store them in the coolest available area. Try to use them soon, since green peppers are difficult to keep any length of time without refrigeration.

- To store eggs without refrigeration, coat the eggs with shortening. It seals out air and preserves them longer.

- By wrapping each citrus fruit individually in aluminum foil, the life of the fruit can be extended. Lemons and oranges can be kept for 2 to 3 months without a noticeable loss of moisture or flavor. Limes seem to keep even longer than lemons.

- If the bananas begin to turn brown before you get around to eating them, put them in the fridge to slow down the ripening process. The cold will kill cells in the skin and make it brown, but the banana inside will stay fresh for several more days.

- Buy potatoes with no evidence of eyes or signs of a green tinge. When potatoes do start to sprout, remove and discard the sprout. Since the potato is a member of the deadly Nightshade family, potato sprouts are lethal.

- Lemon and lime juice, in squeeze bottles where available, are handy for many uses. One Sea Sister pours a bottle of pure lime juice in her water tank each time she fills it. Keeps it fresh tasting. A squirt of lemon juice in each glass of drinking water is also refreshing.

- Some Sea Sisters agree that a vacuum packer can't be beat when it comes to keeping food fresh. Cut vegetables last for weeks. Even mushrooms vacuum packed in a canning jar (the air vacuumed out with the adapter hose that comes with the vac packer) will last that long. Meat, cheese, coffee, bath towels, bed linens, winter sweaters, good jewelry, you name it, can be vac-packed to last nearly indefinitely. Things vac-packed can be stashed in all kinds of spaces with a minimum of space wasted to packing materials!

- Ziploc (twice) all butter and opened cheeses to keep other refrigerator flavors from penetrating these dairy products.

- Also double Ziploc onion and garlic to keep these flavors out of other refrigerated items.

- Did you ever wonder if an egg is good or rotten? Put it in a deep container of cold water. If it floats to the top, it's too old to use.

- No more moldy cheese in the refrigerator: Moisten a paper towel with a bit of cider vinegar and wrap it around the wedge of cheese, then place in a plastic bag and seal. The acid in the vinegar will keep away mold. If the paper towel dries out, dampen it with a bit of water-vinegar solution.

DOES IT NEED REFRIGERATION?

- Margarine (vegetable oil spread) lasts for weeks if not refrigerated. Even if it melts, it just assumes its vegetable oil form.

- Individually wrapped cheese slices keep a long time without benefit of refrigeration, and are available in a wide assortment of fat and cholesterol levels and flavors.

- Cheeses with wax coatings keep for a long time as long as the cover is not punctured or broken.

- Eggs keep for weeks if turned over each week. This keeps the yolk suspended in the white instead of allowing it to settle against the shell where it might deteriorate.

- Dried hard salami, smoked summer sausage and pepperoni sticks, originally purchased unrefrigerated, may be kept that way.

- Country hams are dry-cured with salt and can be stored without refrigeration.

- Try some of the tasty East Indian entree dishes available at the health food stores. No refrigeration is required.

RECOMMENDED GALLEY SUPPLIES

A can crusher eliminates the vast amount of space pop/beer cans quickly consume. This compresses soda cans to 1" instead of six and really saves garbage space, particularly when away from dumpsters for a while. Takes up a little bulkhead space but can be mounted inside a locker or engine compartment to keep it out of the way.

Pack a good knife sharpener. Maybe a pestle and mortar to grind longer-lasting whole spices.

Waterproof matches, a Bic® lighter, a sparklighter—*or all three*—keep the cooking fires burning.

A pressure cooker, 12-volt blender, electric or cast iron fry pan, waffle iron, breadmaker, toaster oven, icemaker, or crock pot seem to be essentials for many boaters. Some of those appliances are brought to the aft deck in order to keep the galley cooler. Good location for a hot plate as well. Seafood cooked outside avoids odors and moisture inside the boat.

Circulon® puts out a fry pan under its *Healthy Cooking By Design* label. Because it is grooved, prepared food has a grilled look, with no need for butter or oil. Marinate the meat overnight, and it will cook perfectly—always moist.

Dazey Seal-A-Meal® packages precooked and frozen dinners, but is also good for sealing paper products, clothing or important papers.

Thermal cups with lids, collapsible 5-gallon containers (water is not always available at the docks), a spare can opener, and a Brita® water filter pitcher will keep you sipping.

Many boaters advise: "Forget the paper plates and plastic everything." They set the table with china, real silverware, cloth napkins, and wine glasses that ding instead of clunk when toasting their successful day at sea.

Many liveaboards and long cruisers can't live without their freezers. A favorite is a bench type on the flybridge, padded to prevent cold derrieres.

Sealable plastic bottles that make ice balls are popular. No worry about spillage.

Most boaters use the non-skid matting for lining cabinets and lockers. Available at marine and discount stores. Works for opening jars, too.

Bring some rubber bands for wrapping around wine glasses that hang upside down. Or use terry cloth wrist bands. It keeps them from clanking/breaking.

A small food grinder, preferably non-rusting, saves time and finger tips. Though not as fast as a food processor, it's better than nothing. Use to gind nuts for baking; conch for fritters; mince clams for chowder; vegetables for whatever.

A collapsible steamer can replace a colander for some uses. It doesn't take up much space, and can be useful for steaming crabs, shrimp lobster, and vegetables.

Standard vacuum bottles keep liquids refreshingly cool for as long as they might stay in the bottle on a hot day. For night watches, available hot water can provide the instant pickup of coffee, hot cocoa, or soup without any of the noisy preparation.

Don't assume that all boat dishes need be plastic. Corning's Corelle plates survive well on a boat, as do some of the heavier ovenware dish sets and coffee mugs.

Real wine glasses can be safely stored upside down in the soft foam-rubber holders made for soft drink cans.

An old-fashioned rotary eggbeater is a useful galley gadget for beating eggs, cake batter, etc.

Miscellaneous utensils might include potato peeler; wire whisk; small grater; 1- or 2–cup sifter; a sieve; a *good* handled can opener.

Instead of a bulky colander which wastes too much space in the galley locker, buy a handled half-circle of plastic with enough holes to allow easy draining (found at Lechters, Wal-Mart, Target, etc.)

Take wooden spoons and plastic forks and spatulas for use with coated cookware.

A wind-up timer. It's too easy to get sidetracked and forget about what you're baking! Can also be used to time long-distance phone calls.

A mallet/meat tenderizer for conch.

Don't forget an ice pick.

An egg slicer can also slice mushrooms or cooked potatoes.

Cardboard matchboxes absorb dampness quickly, and damp matches will not light. Put wooden matches in a jar, and tape sandpaper on the outside for striking the match. Replace the sandpaper when necessary.

Those small, flat pieces of rubber for opening jars that companies often give out as advertising novelties also make great non-slip surfaces under items. They are great for single-handed wine bottle opening, keeping the bottle from turning around with the corkscrew if you use the type of corkscrew with "wings" that come out while you turn the handle on top.

Consider a two-wheel cart for groceries and laundry.

GALLEY STORAGE

- When packing lockers, keep balance in mind. Distribute items so that neither bow nor stern, port nor starboard, is overweight.

- One Sea Sister added an 18" magnetic knife rack, horizontally mounted, to the small space running behind her stove. Be sure to store the long knives so that they will not bother the gas lines. Also be sure to leave enough space, even if the stove is gimbaled.

- Another Sea Sister used the 1 3/4" X 36" counter space behind the fridge and freezer to install a spice rack. Her husband used a piece of flat teak molding, approximately 2" wide, to build a casing, divided it in 2 parts and mounted it to the wall. She made small labels for each cap for easy reading.

- Use small plastic baskets to keep condiments, cheeses, and other small products from shifting in the refrigerator.

- Consider adding smaller shelves at the top of your food storage lockers to store small cans like tomato sauce, tuna or smoked oysters.

- Take as many tight-sealing plastic containers as your boat lockers can hold. Square containers are better than round. Plastic milk containers can be rinsed out and used again.

- Label containers by writing the contents on a mailing label or masking tape with an indelible marker.

- For frequently consumed items (coffee creamer, sugar, rice, oatmeal) use smaller containers and place them near the front of a locker. Refill as needed from the less accessible bulk packages.

- Store items that are sold in glass bottles—such as pickles, sauces, oils, etc—in a plastic dishpan under a seat locker, surrounded by cans, or bubble wrap, or boxed drinks. *Anything* to keep the bottles from touching each other. Breakage should be rare, but the dishpan will confine the mess if this occurs.

- *An exception to storing glass in dishpans is* GLASS BOTTLES OF CLUB SODA. Do not store these at all! Whether it's heat or motion that causes soda to expand, it doesn't just push off the bottle cap; the entire glass bottom may blow off the bottle. Plastic 1-liter bottles are definitely safer.

- One Sea Sister who is cruising in New Zealand found that one gallon plastic jugs worked on her boat as well as Tupperware. She bought mayonnaise jugs from a sandwich deli for 25 cents each, so if she wanted to get rid of them she wouldn't feel bad. Masking tape was used on the lid to indicate what each contained; and the label could be changed at the flick of a wrist. So far they have lasted through four years of cruising.

- Store canned goods by TYPE OF FOOD (soup, meat, fruit, vegetable) and by USUAL USE (lunch, dinner, snack).

- To store the necessary AAA to 9V spare batteries (and extra flashlight bulbs), buy an organizer box (as is used for fish hooks and small tackle).

- Plastic shoe bags, whole or cut to fit, work behind doors or inside cupboards to hold any loose items. Attach with hooks or Velcro, depending on weight.

- You can't have too many waterproof bags.

- Put a dried hot pepper in each jar or plastic bag of dried beans or grains to keep away weevils and other insects. A bay leaf will also thwart weevils.

- Square plastic containers are best for galley foods. They fill space more efficiently than round ones and are recommended for replacing all cardboard to help with garbage and space problems. Cut out the lists of ingredients, cooking directions and included recipes, and tape these to the exterior of the container.

- Bubble wrap or extra tea towels act as buffers for breakables, or simply alternate the glass and the plastic when storing.

- Keep fresh produce cool and dry in hanging nets—or in a food locker containing a frozen gel pack refreshed daily with a frozen spare.

- To protect dried grains and beans from insects during storage, spread a thin layer on a baking sheet and heat for 30 minutes in an oven set from 140° - 160°. Seal in an airtight container.

- Hanging gear hammocks also work well for dirty laundry, kid's toys, and CD's/cassettes.

- Consider mounting a wire mesh holder (covered in vinyl) vertically on the inside of a door to hold Ziploc bags and the electronic match lighter for the stove.

- Luggage straps secure under-settee locker lids for passagemaking. The straps, available at Wal-Mart and elsewhere, are made of webbing and plastic snap buckles. One boater recommends two on each locker. Put the ends around a block of wood, screw the wood to the inside edge of the locker, and pass the straps up and around the lid to snap them together.

- Large plastic underbed containers work well for ease of access. Try stowing under the bridge eyebrow.

- We use stackable and nesting Rubbermaid® containers for carrying items from home. We found this particularly handy when our boat was in charter, and we weren't allowed to keep much on board.

- One Sea Sister uses plastic cups set in her large glasses and then puts the smaller glasses in them to cushion them. She says, "I hate to eat and drink from plastic, and I don't think that you have to give up glass to live on a boat."

- A mini-office box is invaluable. Fill it with stapler and staples, scotch tape, glue, pencils and sharpener, pens, Post-it® notes and small pads, marking pens and highlighters, paper clips, compass, protractor, scissors, rubber bands, and calculator. Non-toxic paint pens work better than the fading "permanent" markers.

- Storage boxes of all sizes for spare parts will keep everything organized. Watch your mate on this one, however, or you may soon need storage boxes for storage boxes.

- To store products (such as liquid soap, bleach, powdered cleansers, rug cleaner, and solvents) use tall plastic baskets or bins. This keeps the products from shifting while underway.

- The cartons from wine coolers or beer six-packs are great organizers for condiments in the galley and odds and ends like flashlights, cans, etc.

- The cost of Tupperware® and Rubbermaid® can gobble up a "cruising kitty." Try using plastic 2-liter drink bottles: terrific storage containers for dog food, dried beans, rice, nuts, etc. Use a funnel to fill the bottle and a layer of Saran Wrap under the lid for an extra seal.

- Porous pottery jugs are quite popular in tropical regions for cooling water without refrigeration. The jugs keep the water cooler than the air temperature because of the tiny amounts of water that seep through the jug and evaporate.

88

- Another method to store cool water is to use a surgical sock, the tubular material a doctor uses under a cast for a broken leg. Pull the fabric over a bottle and saturate with water. Evaporation of the water will cool the contents. A bottle of wine could be quick-chilled by saturating the sock with alcohol.

- Have organized grocery bins: List each item in every grocery bin. When you take an item out, scratch it off. When you put something in, write it down. This way you know what you use and what is in storage. (This might be a tough one for your husband to follow.) Every time food is brought aboard, put it on the food inventory.

- As you store your cans and boxes of groceries, mark the date of purchase on top with a marking pen. This way you can use the oldest groceries first. This takes time, but it is worth it.

- More efficiency in the refrigerator: To keep the cold in a top-loading refrigerator, cut a mylar-foam windshield sunshade to fit the inside top of the refrigerator. As the level of food or drinks decreases, the sunshade isolates the top of the refrigerator from the evaporator or cold-plate, minimizing the volume to be chilled and cutting back on the cycling of the compressor.

MORE GALLEY TIPS FROM WOMEN ABOARD

- There's no need to throw away and replace rubber non-skid when it gets dirty. Just throw it in the washing machine and it'll be good as new.

- Use a meat baster to "squeeze" your pancake batter onto the hot griddle- perfect shaped pancakes every time.

- When a recipe calls for a small quantity of juice, don't cut the lemon. Just puncture it with an ice pick, then gently squeeze. Wrap the lemon in foil and store for future use.

- To easily remove burnt on food from your skillet, simply add a drop or two of dish soap and enough water to cover bottom of pan, and bring to a boil on stove-top-skillet will be much easier to clean now.

- Spray your Tupperware with nonstick cooking spray before pouring in tomato-based sauces—no more stains.

- Before squeezing a lemon, submerge it in hot water for 15 minutes. You'll get more juice out of it.

- THINK before going into the fridge or ice box so that everything can be gotten out at the same time. Gather together items to go back in so that they can be replaced at the same time. AND if you can try to always put categories of things (butter, cheese, leftovers, pickles) back in the same general part of the fridge you will save on searching time with the door open.

- When provisioning for a long trip, the "bulk-buying" panic may set in. Resist the temptation and plan your storage wisely. A case of toilet paper may seem like a good deal until you open the box and have to rewrap each roll individually to keep out dampness. Same with paper towels. Canned goods in their smallest cans can be tucked into nooks and crannies where the "industrial-size" won't fit. Plus, you won't have to worry about what to do with what's left over.

- For easy clean-up, spray a grater with vegetable cooking spray before grating cheese or orange rind.

- Proper use of pots and pans can help your range save on energy. Fit the pot or pan to the burner, since a small pot or pan on a large element wastes heat, and a large pot on a small element is inefficient.

- Put a lid on the pan you're using to boil water since it will boil faster, saving up to 20% of the energy that otherwise would be consumed.

- It's important to keep pan bottoms clean because a layer of soot decreases heating efficiency on any type of stove. Shiny pans are particularly efficient in electric cooking.

- If your coffee is too bitter from being heated too long, just toss in a pinch of salt to banish the bitter taste.

- Go to thrift shops and buy measuring cups, just the odd ones that they have, and put them in your containers to measure without having to pull out the set of measuring cups.

- To prevent water from in coming through the thru-hull and splashing out of the sink while on a port or starboard tack, try placing a small plate over the drain (instead of closing off the thru-hull). The plate allows water to drain when you use the sink, but keeps incoming water from splashing onto the cabinets and towels. A stopper pops out with wave action.

- To eliminate suds from a sink when it comes time to rinse the dishes, sprinkle salt on the suds.

- You've probably noticed that dish soaps are coming out in "boat size" containers. Not only do you use less (they're concentrated), but the containers are handy to recycle for fabric softener, bleach, laundry soap, etc.

- Store sponges, scrubbers and other cleaning implements in a strawberry basket attached to a cup hook screwed into the wall behind the sink.

- Never buy cheap trash bags. One bumpy trip in the dinghy should be enough to convince.

- Paper towels being unwrapped by the breeze blowing through your galley? A hat/corsage pin (bought in packages in the fabric section of Wal-Mart for a dollar or two) stuck through the paper will control them. Painting the head of the pin with fingernail polish will make it much more visible.

- Haven't yet installed the paper towel holder? Consider installing it vertically on the wall, rather than horizontally. For some reason, that seems to make the towels less likely to unroll.

- When chopping onions, breathe only through your opened mouth. Your eyes will never fill with tears!

- You'll shed fewer tears when peeling and chopping onions if you chill them thoroughly in the refrigerator beforehand.

- To enable catsup to flow out evenly, first insert a drinking straw, pushing it all the way to the bottom of the bottle, and remove it. A bit of air is all it takes to release the vacuum and allow the ketchup to flow easily.

91

- Use clothespins to close bags of snacks.

- Try using spring-loaded curtain rods in your refrigerator to keep items on the shelves during rough passages.

- Give frozen fish a desirable fresh flavor by thawing it in milk. The milk eliminates the frozen taste.

- Make any fish taste tender and sweet by soaking it in 1/4 cup of lemon juice and water, or vinegar, or wine before cooking.

- After handling fish, eliminate the odor on your hands by rubbing them with salt or vinegar.

- A Sea Sister writes, "Whenever I try a new recipe, I always write: 1) the date; 2) any comments; 3) any ingredients I might have changed or added to make it better; and 4) the place we were when I tried it. Now, looking through my cookbooks brings back some nice memories."

- Fish won't stick to the pan during baking if you lay it on a bed of parsley, celery, and chopped onions. This vegetable bed also adds flavor.

- Economize on time and fuel by steaming two vegetables simultaneously in the same pot. If you want to serve them separately, loosely wrap each in aluminum foil during cooking.

- To make frozen vegetables taste as much as possible like fresh ones, pour boiling water on them before cooking. This flushes away all traces of frozen water.

- Place salad greens in a plastic bag, add the dressing, and shake the entire mixture. The greens will be evenly coated on both sides.

- Jars that hold instant coffee, powdered creamer, sugar, and other dry foods will stay airtight longer if a small piece of plastic wrap or a sandwich bag is used as a gasket to help seal the lid.

- USES FOR FOIL WINE BAGS (inside boxed wine.) Wash them and refill with any liquid. They take up less space, won't leak, and conform to fit into lockers or refrigerators.

92

⇒ to store used engine oil until a proper oil waste dump can be located;

⇒ blown up and used as a float for swimming;

⇒ inflated slightly for use as a seat cushion at the bull fights (Can you tell this cruiser was in Mexico?)

⇒ cut in strips and assembled around lead and a fish hook—great mahi mahi lure!

⇒ refilled with cheap bottled wine when boxed wine isn't available (easier storage);

⇒ filled with water and frozen, then placed on top of freezer or cold plate to help retard cold air loss, or placed in an ice chest (as the ice melts, the bag retains the water, thereby allowing the other contents to remain dry);

⇒ makes great heating pads for those occasional aches and pains;

⇒ inflated slightly and used as padding between breakables in a locker.

TRIED AND TRUE PRODUCTS

- VIGO'S 1-STEP NOODLES are worth trying! Saves water, propane, aggravation, and time.

- MOTT'S JUICE CONCENTRATE in a 12 oz. aluminum can makes 48 ounces. No refrigeration needed, easy to store, and no leakage like the paper concentrate containers.

- READY-CRISP bacon from SHK Foods, Madison, WI. No refrigeration needed until package is opened. Pre-cooked and vacuum-sealed. You can eat it right from the pouch, or microwave (10 seconds per slice). Just think: BLT's, filet mignon, hot bacon dressing, German potato salad! No grease. No mess. Less galley time!

- PARMALAT is a brand of milk that has about a six-month shelf life without refrigeration. You can find this all over the Bahamas as well as in the U.S. Whole, 2%, 1% and non-fat milks are available at Publix for $.99 . Usually it's in the same section as powdered milk. Of course, after opening it requires refrigeration.

- NIDO, by Nestlés, is dry, whole milk. Cruisers say it takes great!

- HOLSUM'S BAHAMA BREAD lasts a long time before loaf mildews.

- One Sea Sister recommends "Whitecaps in the Icebox" by Lynn Ove Mortensen, (Evergreen Pacific Publishing, Seattle Washington c. 1990) as a good onboard cookbook. It was written by a woman sailor cruising in the Pacific Northwest, and contains lots of tips, in addition to good recipes.

- California Innovations sells a collapsible cooler called a THERMALWHIZ. The 36-can size has a plastic zip-out lining to be used if you are carrying ice/cold items. Remove the lining to carry hot items. Velcro straps hold it in its collapsed state. We had read about it in Practical Sailor and found it at Target for $20.00. There are several sizes, but this one has both the hot and cold insulation.

- One of our Sea Sisters wrote to tell about a custom-made insulation pad that went across the top of her refrigerator. It can also be used in top-loading ice boxes. It is very thin and easily bent to accommodate getting under to retrieve what you want on either side of the lid (if your reefer is designed that way). You do want to take accurate measurements and consider whether or not you want the pad to extend beyond the opening. The company that makes this "Super Q Ice Saver Blanket" is Standout Yacht Fittings, 2101 N. Steele Street, Tacoma, WA 98406; phone 800-622-1877. The price was very reasonable and the order handled quite promptly. As an added plus, they make a number of other products, especially out of Sunbrella, that she was not aware of until receiving a brochure with her order.

- Nice-looking, completely enclosed dispensers designed to store your tin foil, wax paper, and plastic wrap may be ordered from a boating catalogue called *Welcome Aboard*, 800-295-2469.

- One Sea Sister found a great bargain—CONSOLIDATED PLASTICS CO., INC. from Ohio offers industrial containers, trays, and storage boxes at discount prices. The more you order, the greater the discount. Storage boxes are Rubbermaid® and come in all sizes and shapes. Call 800-362-1000 and ask for their catalogs (Industrial, Bags; Packing & Shipping Supplies, Commercial Matting).

- Boboli® pizza crusts provide versatility, require no refrigeration, and take only a few minutes in the oven. Be inventive on your toppings—anything goes from leftover grilled veggies, a jar of artichokes or green chilies.

94

- Liquid sugar substitute mixed 50/50 with regular sugar is hard to tell from the real stuff. Takes up far less room, and won't clump.

- One boater says tortillas will keep a month unrefrigerated, even in the tropics, or four months if cold. She also claims bottled Recaito® by Goya, found in the Mexican section of the grocery, is a great substitute for fresh cilantro. For a good salsa, try Rotel® tomatoes, chopped onion, and Recaito®.

- Couscous is quick to cook and some find it more interesting than traditional rice.

* * *

ZIPLOC® STORAGE BAGS, invented almost 30 ago, ranks high on most provisioning lists, and well they should! Two-gallon sizes are handy for toilet paper and two-pack paper towels. Smaller sizes work well for protecting passports and valuable papers, holding tiny parts, and leaving messages on boats.

If you wish to protect against rust, sew some granular silica into a small cloth pouch and insert it, with whatever you are protecting, into a Ziploc. Close the bag, then slip a straw through the seal and suck out the extra air. Quickly withdraw the straw and re-seal, then tape the bag closed.

But uses for Ziplocs extend beyond than just storing and marinating food and keeping your paper products dry. For instance:

- MAKING POTPOURRI. Collect dried roses, juniper sprigs, tiny pinecones, strips of orange rind, bay leaves, cinnamon sticks, whole cloves, and allspice berries. Mix a few drops of rose, cinnamon, and balsam oils with orris root (available at your local crafts store). Add all ingredients and seal in a Ziploc for a few weeks to mellow. Be sure to turn the bag occasionally.

- STORE SMALL CRAFTS ITEMS. Buttons, beads and various odds and ends store well in Ziplocs.

- CLEANING SHOWER HEADS. If a shower head cannot be easily removed for cleaning, fill a Ziploc with vinegar, wrap it around the shower head, and secure in place overnight with a rubber band.

- ORGANIZING CLOTHES AND JEWELRY. Lingerie, scarves, gloves, socks, and handkerchiefs. Also rings, earrings, necklaces, pins.

- ICING ON THE CAKE. Fill a pint-size Ziploc with icing, twist the bag to force icing to one corner, seal, and use scissors to snip a small bit off the corner. Squeeze out icing to make polka dots, squiggles, or write names. Use a separate bag for each color.

- SNACKS. Whether you're traveling in the car, hiking, or taking a float trip, pack snacks in Ziplocs. Also, pack a wet wash cloth for clean-up afterwards.

- STORING SEEDS. Seal seeds in Ziplocs and put them in a cool, dry place until they're ready to be planted.

- STORING GAME PIECES. Never lose dice, cards, or playing pieces again.

- IMPORTANT PAPERS. Protect important papers by storing tax forms, important records, cancelled checks, receipts, warranties, and instructions. They're also useful for storing BILLS TO BE PAID, especially in humid areas that can seal an envelope before its time.

- SEASONAL ITEMS. Pack leftover holiday greeting cards and decorations.

- PACKING. Store maps, medications, toiletries, and first aid supplies.

- IN THE WORKSHOP. Organize nuts, bolts, drill bits, nails, washer, and screws.

PESTS ONBOARD

The importance of keeping roaches off your boat and out of your galley goes without saying. Particularly in warm climates, get in the habit of NOT bringing boxes aboard for any length of time, if at all. Instead, unpack and repackage items on the dock if possible. This goes for EVERYTHING that is packaged in boxes: grocery items, boat and automotive parts, packages that are shipped to you. In spite of your good intentions, however, these stowaway experts may infiltrate your galley. Here's what you can do:

SUBSTITUTIONS FOR ROACH REPELLANT
What to use instead:

- **BAY LEAVES.** Researchers at Kansas State University were able to validate this folk remedy in 1982 by showing that bay leaves repelled cockroaches in insect tanks. The active ingredient in the leaves is *cineaole* (also known as eucalyptol). A bay leaf in your flour canister should keep the flour free from bugs. Place bay leaves wherever you have a problem: in the pantry, cupboards, shelves.

- **CHEAP WINE.** Put saucers of it under your cabinets. Roaches love it, crawl in, drink it, get tipsy, and drown!

- **SODA.** The easiest roach trap is to leave some soda inside a soda can. You can't see the roaches too readily, but you'll *hear* them. A glass jar, preferably one with a narrow taper at the top, gets the same results. Bugs jump in after the food and cannot climb out the slippery sides. (CAUTION: You might want to somehow mark the can and identify its use, so that some unsuspecting person doesn't accidentally take a swig of the soda!)

- The **CUCUMBER** is an effective cockroach chaser. Place cucumber skins wherever you have a roach problem. The vegetable's repellent quality comes from a naturally occurring compound in the plant called "trans-2-nonenal."

- **ROACH COOKIES** - Mix boric acid with bacon grease. If the mixture is a little runny, add enough flour so that the consistency is similar to biscuit dough. Roll into little balls and generously place under cabinets, under floor boards, etc. (The balls will harden.)

- **ROACH COOKIES** - Another recipe calls for 8 teaspoons of POWDERED BORIC ACID (available at most pharmacies in 12 oz. containers) and 3 teaspoons of SWEETENED CONDENSED MILK. Drop by small amounts onto a dish or cookie sheet covered with wax paper. (Makes 6-8 cookies.) Harden by placing in a sunny spot. After the cookies harden, leave the wax paper under them and cut around each one. Place individual cookies around the boat in areas where roaches might nest, especially the galley.

CLEANING TIPS FROM *WOMEN ABOARD*

One Sea Sister wrote, "When on an extended cruise especially, I don't have room to carry a supply of window cleaner, oven cleaner, toilet bowl cleaner, tile cleaner, floor cleaner, rug cleaner, upholstery cleaner, sink cleaner, drain cleaner, degreaser, spray for dusting furniture, furniture polish, metal polishes, etc. So I mix my own, using ingredients that I normally carry onboard anyway. The following recipes are less toxic and hazardous than most household cleaners available on the grocery store shelf. They are also less costly."

- ALL-PURPOSE CLEANER - Combine 1 tsp. vegetable oil-based liquid soap, 1 tsp. borax, 1 qt. warm water, and 1 Tbsp. distilled white vinegar (or lemon juice)

- CHROME POLISH - Apple cider vinegar

- DRAIN CLEANER - Pour in 1/2 cup baking soda, followed by 1/2 cup distilled white vinegar. Close drain and wait 5 minutes. Pour in tea kettle of boiling water. Repeat as needed.

- FLOOR CLEANER - (For lasting shine on wood, tile, or linoleum) 1/8 cup vegetable-based detergent, 1/2 cup distilled white vinegar, and 2 gallons warm water.

98

- FURNITURE/WOOD DUSTING - Mix 1/2 tsp. olive oil, 1/4 cup distilled white vinegar or lemon juice and apply to cotton cloth. Reapply as necessary.

- FURNITURE POLISH - Almond or linseed oil. Or a mixture of sewing machine oil and mineral spirits (half & half) in a spray bottle.

- GREASE REMOVAL - Borax on a damp cloth

- NON-ABRASIVE CLEANSER - Combine 1/4 cup baking soda and enough vegetable-based detergent to make a creamy paste.

- OVEN CLEANER - Mix 2 Tbsp. liquid soap and 2 tsp. borax with warm water.

- RUG OR CARPET CLEANER - Club soda

- SCOURING POWDER - Baking soda and salt

- TOILET BOWL CLEANER - Paste of borax and lemon juice, or if you prefer, pour 1 cup borax into toilet bowl, let set overnight, flush in the morning. Stains and rings are lifted out.

- TUB AND TILE CLEANER - 1/4 cup baking soda plus 1/2 cup distilled white vinegar mixed with water.

- EXTRA-STRENGTH ALL-PURPOSE CLEANER - Mix 1/4 cup baking soda, 1/2 cup white vinegar, 3/4 cup household ammonia, and 1 gallon warm water.

- SCOURING POWDER - Combine 1/4 cup baking soda, 1/4 cup borax, 1-1/2 cups hot water.

- WOOD FURNITURE/FLOOR POLISH - Combine 1/2 cup white vinegar, 1/2 cup vegetable or mineral oil, and 1 Tbsp. lemon juice. Mix well. Rub on surface. Buff with clean, dry cloth.

- FURNITURE POLISH - Combine 3 Tbsp. lemon juice and 1 quart vegetable or mineral oil. Wipe on with a cloth. Remove with a clean cloth.

- COPPER CLEANER - Rub with vinegar and salt.

- SILVER POLISH - Mix 2 Tbsp. baking soda and 1 Tbsp. salt. Pour on a small piece of aluminum foil. Soak silver for 1 hour. Wash normally.

- MILDEW REMOVER - Spray mildew with hydrogen peroxide. Scrub with a thick paste of lemon juice and borax to inhibit new mildew formation.

- VARNISHED ITEMS - Leftover tea makes a good cleaning agent for varnished items.

- BRASS - Use ketchup to clean brass. Smear it on, let set a bit, rinse and dry.

- COPPER AND BRASS CLEANER - To clean brass and copper, make a paste of salt, vinegar, and flour. Leave polish on an hour or so; then rub off with a soft cloth; wash.

- DISCOLORED ITEMS - Use salt as a scouring powder for discolored coffee mugs and pots.

- SCRATCHES ON WOOD - Liquid shoe polish or walnut or pecan meat can be used to cover scratches in finished wood.

- WINDOW CLEANER - Mix 1/4 cup distilled white vinegar to 1 quart warm water. Or, shake up 1/2 tsp. liquid soap, 3 Tbsp. vinegar and 2 cups of water in a spray bottle.

- DISTILLED WHITE VINEGAR - Add half a cup of vinegar to a quart of water.

- AMMONIA - Add 1 Tablespoon to a quart of warm water (wear protective gloves.)

- Here's one Sea Sister's formula for washing those sea-salt spots off your windows! Mix in a bucket of warm water:
  1 cup white vinegar
  1/2 cup ammonia
  2 Tbsp. cornstarch

100

Use a clean sponge (her designated-window sponge resides in its own marked Ziploc bag) and simply wipe the solution on your windows—no elbow grease needed! Dry with a paper towel and your windows will sparkle!

Everybody says, "Cornstarch???" but this Sea Sister says, "It's unbelievable. It really works!"

* * *

Products that have multiple uses on board are the most welcome. **CLOROX BLEACH**, invented in 1916, is one of the staples. Here are just a few of its uses:

<u>Mildew</u>: Place all the bathroom accessories into a large bucket or pan, fill with two gallons water, and add one and a half cups Clorox Bleach. Rinse and drain.

To clean mildew out of your grout, mix 3/4 cup Clorox to one gallon of water, and use an old toothbrush.

<u>Disinfecting garbage cans</u>: Wash the garbage cans with a solution made with 3/4 cup of Clorox to 1 gallon water. Let stand for five minutes, and rinse clean.

<u>Freshen galley sponges</u>: Soak sponges for 5-10 minutes in a mixture of 3/4 cup bleach per gallon of water. Rinse well.

<u>Prolong the life of fresh flowers</u>, add 1/4 teaspoon (20 drops) of Clorox to each quart of water used in your vase.

<u>Clean white appliances</u> by mixing 3/4 cup Clorox to 1 gallon of water, applying with a sponge. Let stand for 10 minutes. Then rinse and dry thoroughly.

<u>Clean butcher block cutting boards</u> to prevent bacterial from breeding by washing the cutting board with hot, sudsy water and rinse clean. Then apply a solution of 3 Tablespoons Clorox per gallon of water. Keep wet for 2 minutes, then rinse completely.

<u>Remove coffee and tea stains</u> by soaking clean cups for 5-10 minutes in a solution of 1 Tablespoon of bleach with each gallon of water.

To make a funnel, cut an empty, clean Clorox bottle in half, remove the cap, and keep it under your sink.

To clean a rubber sink or bath mat, fill the sink or tub with water, add one-quarter cup of Clorox, and soak the mat 5-10 minutes.

Clean thermos bottles with diluted Clorox, then rinse.

An empty Clorox bottle makes a great boat buoy. Cap the empty bottle tightly, tie a rope to the handle, and tie a weight to the other end of the rope. These buoys can also be strung together to mark swimming areas.

MORE CLEANING TIPS

- For burned- or baked-on food, mix 2 Tbsp. liquid dish washing detergent with 3 tsp. baking soda. Add ingredients to enough water to cover the burned-on food. Boil for 15-20 minutes. Wash normally.

- Oven cleaner: Scour your oven with baking soda. If your oven has a spill, sprinkle salt on it while still warm and then clean by hand.

- Aluminum pot cleaner: Mix 2 pints of water with 3 Tbsp. white vinegar. Bring ingredients to a boil, and continue to boil until stains are gone.

- One Sea Sister uses Pledge to clean her stainless steel sinks. Cleans the grime and leaves a shine!

- KEEPING FENDERS CLEAN: One Sea Sister said that when they brought their boat to Houston, they put 3 or 4 trash bags on their fenders when they were in the locks which helped them continue looking like new.

- TOPSIDES: Use cleaner made for white-wall tires.

- The easiest and most economical way one Annapolis Sea Sister found to clean the brown "mustache," off of the hull (particularly near the bow) is to use a 50% solution of MURIATIC ACID. This can be purchased in a hardware store by the quart ($1.89) or gallon ($2.20.) It is used to clean concrete and brick, but also to adjust proper pH in swimming pools, so don't let it scare you.

Mix a quart bottle of 1/2 Muriatic Acid and 1/2 water and store in a acid proof container. When a "mustache" appears on your hull, get out your acid solution, a sponge mop, bucket, and hose. Pour a small amount (1/4" to 1/2") of solution in the bucket, enough to wet the sponge mop a few times. Wet the mop with solution and apply to the brown spots. Wait a few minutes and it magically disappears. Rinse well with clean water. Usually this can be done from the deck by hanging over the rail, but we find it easier to just hop into the water and apply from there.

A few cautions:

> ➤ Don't leave the solution on for long
> ➤ Rinse right after the brown fades
> ➤ Don't get this on your skin as it will burn (rinse immediately if you do).

"My husband discovered this after years of people talking about using "Tidy Bowl" toilet cleaner to clean their hulls. Muriatic acid is the main ingredient at a fraction of the price. Our chemist friend explains that it works because this stain is chiefly organic and the acid kills the little organisms clinging to the hull. I like it because it's the closest thing to a magic trick you can perform while cleaning your boat."

• LAUNDRY SOAP and BLEACH serve more purposes than you think. Plastic bags of detergent are good trading stock (as are powdered milk and cooking oil). Bleach is handy to soak suspicious veggies in.

• A one-gallon size WET/DRY VACUUM should keep your quarters shipshape. And stock old rags in abundance.

• A SMALL WHISK BROOM that snaps into a tiny dustpan works great for little jobs.

TIPS FOR YOUR HEAD

• As an important part of your head maintenance schedule: Add one quart of Heinz vinegar to your head bowl and flush (on dry cycle) until the vinegar disappears from the bowl. Allow the vinegar to stand in the plumbing lines for 12-24 hours, then use the head normally. Vinegar helps clear lines of salt and calcium deposits which create blockage. Add 1/2 cup vegetable oil or commercial head lube. Flush until oil disappears from bowl; then allow to sit overnight. (**IMPORTANT: NEVER use Clorox in your marine head!!!!** It is extremely damaging to the sanitation hose lining and will result in severe malodor problems.)

- For regular head cleaning: Sprinkle baking soda into head and brush.

- For stains: Mix 1/3 cup lemon juice with 2/3 cup borax to made a paste. Flush head to wet sides. Coat the stains with the paste. Let sit for 1-2 hours. Scrub head with brush.

- Vinegar is great for cleaning soap scum, mildew, and grime from bathtubs, tiles, and shower curtains. Simply wipe the surface with the vinegar and rinse with water.

- Unclogging a shower head: Unscrew the shower head, remove the rubber washer, place the head in a pot filled with equal parts vinegar and water, bring to a boil, then simmer for 5 minutes.

- A Sea Sister writes, "Because we have two heads, we store a broom and our feather duster behind the door in the forward one, hung by those little clips. I also have a five bar hanger on the back of the door that houses my belts (good for ties too). Yes, we will have to remove it if a guest wants to use the shower, but hey, we live here more than we have guests."

TRIED AND TRUE PRODUCTS

- WINK is an inexpensive product you can buy in the grocery store. You will find the brown bottle with white printing in the soap and cleaners aisle. WINK takes out rust stains from a white deck and also from clothes.

- GOO-GONE is a liquid solvent that will take any sticky substances off a wall, bottle, or any other surface. WD-40 works well, too.

- RUBBERMAID SHELF LINER is a good product to keep glasses and other things from shifting in storage cabinets. Use it under liquor bottles and canisters to keep them from sliding on cabinets. Different sizes can be cut for drink coasters, place mats, stand-up picture frames, and flower arrangements.

- One Sea Sister used Scott's LIQUID GOLD for the past 2½ years on her interior teak. She found it <u>unsatisfactory</u> because it attracted dust and needed to be reapplied every week or so. She then discovered Ace Hardware's TUNG OIL FINISH. After cleaning the teak with a deep cleansing furniture cleaning, the Tung Oil is applied. It contains bee's wax, really looks beautiful, and lasts for ages! It comes in two finishes; she uses the gloss."

- Another Sea Sister was so excited to discover a WATER-BASED VARNISH that is available through Woodworker Supply, 1-800-645-9292. Catalog #915380: Water-based varnish, satin. Catalog #915387: Water-based varnish, gloss. The cost per quart is $21.95.

- INFLATABLE TIP: *Never* use products containing silicone (such as Armor All) to restore hypalon or PVC inflatable boats. The product to use after cleaning is **303**. This product contains a UV protectant. It is excellent for cleaning and protecting the vinyl windows in cockpit enclosures, as well.

- Another product that I am simply in love with is BOAT ARMOR HEAVY DUTY UNIVERSAL MARINE CLEANER. This is the only cleaner that I've found that works as advertised. Use it primarily to clean tough dirt on everything—fiberglass, canvas, rubber, carpet, teak, vinyl, glass, stainless steel. It works particularly well on fenders and canvas.

- BABY WIPES are like a quick shower in a box. They save on water and washcloths, plus before tossing them, you can take a swipe at the sink, commode, or floor.

- JOY® dishwashing liquid lathers in salt water, and doubles as a bilge and sump sweetener.

- To break up the grease that builds in a gray water sump, pour a little Fantastik® down the drain every week or so.

- SNOBOL® liquid disinfectant works well on rust stains anywhere on the boat, particularly on stainless or fiberglass. Its active ingredient is hydrochloric acid, so use with extreme care and remove quickly.

- Use SOFT SCRUB® with bleach for an all around cleaner. Let it sit if the stain is stubborn.

- Try GREASED LIGHTNING®, a non-abrasive, non-toxic, biodegradable product for slimy bilge sludge. (In close quarters, *non-toxic* is a good word.)

- GUNK® Hand Cleaner does the trick when you come out of the engine room.

- GOO GONE gets rid of stickers, grease, gum, tar, crayon, and tape.

- NU FINISH POLISH keeps the rust spots and salt spots off far longer than just chrome polish/metal cleaner alone. Comes in an orange plastic bottle and can be found in many supermarkets (auto section), hardware stores and auto supply stores.

In the Engine Rooms of *WOMEN ABOARD*

For nearly two and half years, we were extremely fortunate to have articles on diesel engine maintenance contributed by BECKY O'CAIN of Diesel Engine and Parts Company in Houston, Texas.

Becky had the gift of being able to explain something seemingly foreign and complex to our Sea Sisters, and introduced many of us to the wonders of the engine room. Her advice was well-researched and each month her columns were as eagerly anticipated by Sea Sisters as by their husbands or significant others.

While writing for us, Becky accepted a job promotion and suddenly her home and work responsibilities took priority to her articles, as well they should. We are grateful for the time she gave us, and we miss her wit and expertise terribly.

Here is the complete collection of **FROM THE ENGINE ROOMS OF WOMEN ABOARD**, written by Becky O'Cain, November 1994 to April 1997.

WINTER STORAGE PROCEDURES

For those of you who do not live on or use your boat year-round, winter can be very tough on your engine unless steps are taken to prevent Jack Frost from taking his toll. Winterizing an engine is not as critical in the south as it is for our Sisters in the northern part of the country, but winter is an excellent time to do preventive maintenance in anticipation of the warmer weather and heavier use.

The first and most important step is to <u>check the freeze protection of your anti-freeze.</u> Start the engine and bring it up to operating temperature and use an antifreeze tester (available in most auto parts stores.) Please use caution when checking the cooling system. The water will be extremely hot. The solution of ethylene glycol base permanent antifreeze should be enough to protect your engines from freeze-up during the coldest part of winter. In high performance engines, the ratio of anti-freeze to water should not be more than 50-50. Believe it or not, an excessive amount of anti-freeze *adversely* affects freeze protection and heat transfer rates.

<u>Check all hoses and clamps.</u> Worn hoses should be replaced.

Drain the raw water system. Be sure the raw water is drained from the lowest position in the system. Remove the raw water pump cover (refer to your owner's manual for location of pump on your particular engine) and the impeller. Removing the impeller is important because during an extended storage time, the blade of the impeller bent against the cam could set and be permanently damaged.

Change the oil and oil filter. (Before adding new oil, be sure you have replaced and tightened the oil pan drain plug or a major, oily mess will occur. Don't laugh; even experienced mechanics sometimes forget to do this!) After changing, run the engine long enough to make sure all moving components have been coated.

Completely fill the fuel tanks. This prevents water from entering the system from condensation. Replace fuel filters. Follow the procedure in your owner's manual for "filling" (or priming) the fuel filter. Start and operate the engine for about five minutes to circulate the clean fuel.

Drain and replace your marine gear (transmission) oil. Again, refer to your owner's manual for the correct type and grade of oil to use. Start and run the engine at idle RPM for ten minutes to coat the internal parts with clean oil. Engage the clutch and alternate from forward to reverse to circulate clean oil throughout all the moving parts.

Remove and clean the batteries and battery cables. Use a baking soda and water solution to do this, but be careful not to let the solution enter the battery. Add distilled water to the batteries, if necessary. Store the batteries where the temperature will not fall below freezing. Keep the batteries fully charged through the winter. You may want to also loosen your alternator belts. This will prevent sticking between the belt and pulley.

Seal all engine openings, such as the air intakes and exhaust outlets. You can use a water resistant tape, or better yet, cardboard, plywood or metal covers, if possible.

This is also a good time to completely clean the exterior of the engine to check for areas that show corrosion, and use some touch up spray paint to prevent further rust and corrosion.

FUELISH FACTS

There are just about as many fuel treatment products on the market as there are fuel docks. How do you know which ones are right for you? I'll try to dispel some of the myths and mysteries about your diesel fuel and the products the manufacturers recommend you use.

The current "buzz word" in the fuel business is *low sulfur fuel*. Let's talk a little about that. Sulfur is a natural lubricant in diesel fuel. With the current mandates governing the level of sulfur in fuel, the lubricity of diesel fuel has diminished significantly. The lack of lubricity can cause excessive and early wear on fuel pumps and injection systems. In order to prevent this wear, a lubricity additive should be used. There are several brands on the market at very low costs (a pint can treat 200-250 gallons of fuel depending on the brand). The cost for a pint should not be over about $7.00.

Water in the fuel is another concern. Water does not burn, and water in your fuel can cause the fuel to burn slower and possibly not burn at all. This causes a loss in power and engine efficiency. The unburned and partially-burned fuel escapes through the exhaust system which damages the environment, as well as being cause for alarm to the engine operator as it is *visible* exhaust. It can also cause corrosion in your fuel lines, etc. The major sources of water being introduced into fuel is seepage into storage tanks and condensation in the engine fuel system. Basically, I'm telling you it cannot be prevented, but it can be minimized. There are special filtration systems and additives that can help to eliminate the problem. Again, if you use an additive, a small amount will treat several hundred gallons of fuel.

Let's not forget about bacteria. Bacteria thrive in the engine environment. They grow rapidly at high temperatures. They can cause corrosion, slime, odor and deposits in your entire fuel system from the tank to the exhaust. You may think this treatment to be a little pricey in the beginning, but bear in mind that a 16-ounce bottle will treat almost 2,000 gallons of fuel! This treatment is a periodic treatment, not a constant one.

There are many more products on the market that could be beneficial in your particular application. Take the time to research these products thoroughly before you make the decision to use them. A reputable service outlet should be willing to provide you with all the information you need. If not, let me know and I'll be more than happy to help you make a decision or recommend a brand name.

109

AIR FILTERS

Let's talk about air filters. Everyone knows (or should know) that filters should be changed at regular intervals. Some of you, however, may be changing your air filters TOO often!

First, let's look at why it is important for the air entering your engine to be clean. In the combustion process, air is mixed with the fuel to achieve combustion. This happens in the cylinders. Just like dirt in your oil or fuel, dirt or dust in the air can create problems that, in the long run, could result in the need for a major overhaul costing thousands of dollars. When combustion occurs, the particles of dust and dirt remain unburned and "drop" into the cylinder walls creating "scores" or scratches in the cylinder liner and piston. This creates excessive wear on the piston rings, causing fuel to escape unburned and allowing dirt to drop into the oil pan. The dirt will continue to move throughout the engine causing wear to any moving part, which can cause high oil consumption, inefficient operation and decreased power. Thus, the inevitable overhaul.

Now, I'm really going to confuse you. Did you know that as an air filter is used and becomes dirty, the filter's efficiency actually INCREASES? I can hear you now. "Becky, that contradicts everything you just said!!" Well, yes and no. Here's how it works: As soon as the air filter is put into operation, it begins to remove harmful particles. As these particles accumulate throughout the filter medium, the small openings in the medium become smaller, thus allowing the filter to trap finer dust particles. See how that works? The trick is to know when the filter is too dirty.

You cannot tell how dirty an air cleaner is by simply looking at it. The easiest way to tell is with an *air restriction indicator*. Your owner's manual should have a section which addresses the maximum degree of vacuum in the air induction system that the engine can tolerate and still operate efficiently. A restriction indicator, installed between the engine and the filter, will measure this vacuum. They are inexpensive and very easy to read and understand. For less than $20, you can save yourself thousands in the long run.

I would still recommend that you replace your air filter once a year regardless of what the indicator may say. Moisture, vibration and temperature deviations can cause the media (the "stuff" inside the filter) to deteriorate. If you do not have an indicator, a good rule of thumb is to replace your air filter with every third oil and oil filter change.

Here are some simple Do's and Don'ts to remember:

1 Don't take the air cleaner out to look at it or inspect it. This can do more harm than good.
2 Always use the correct element. Even a fraction of an inch makes a difference.
3 Never rap a filter in an attempt to remove the trapped dirt. This can damage the filter which can allow dirt to bypass it, thus creating more problems.
4 Before removing the air cleaner cover, wipe away any dirt or dust that could drop into the engine.
5 Check the gaskets and seals around the cleaner. Make sure there are no signs of leakage or "dust patterns" that could indicate leaks.
6 When taking the old cleaner out, do it carefully. A bump could cause dirt to drop.
7 Using a moist cloth, wipe the inside of the filter housing before installing the new filter.
8 Do not wash your filter and reuse it. The efficiency will not be as good, and damage—although not visually evident—could occur.
9 If there is any evidence of damage to the new filter, do not use it.
10 As always, follow your engine manufacturer's guidelines.

If you feel your air filter usage is too high, contact your engine manufacturer. The reason could be very simple.

GETTING YOUR BOAT READY FOR THE SEASON

It's the time of year when those of you who have had your boats in storage (or idle) throughout the winter think about reversing
winterizing process. You may want to refer to the article on winterizing to remind yourselves what was recommended.

• First of all, remove all the covers and tape from the engine openings. (Be sure fuel tank vents are open.)

• Charge the stored batteries and install. Make sure you securely fasten the cables. Tighten the alternator belt to the proper tension.

• Change the oil and oil filters. The oil used during storage should be considered basically a "preservative" oil for winter. If you have a turbocharged engine, use an oil can to pre-lube the turbocharger

111

bearings. While you are oiling the bearings, turn the turbo by hand (the little "fins" inside).

- Close all the drains that were open on the raw water system. Install the raw water pump impeller. Make sure you have the impeller on in the right direction. Install the water pump cover, using a new gasket. Remove the plug on the suction side of the raw water pump. This is so you can prime the pump. It's a good idea not to start the engine while the pump is dry. This could cause impeller damage. Reinstall the plug. Check the level of the antifreeze and make sure all hoses are tight.

- Prime the engine with clean diesel fuel. If you can, rotate the engine 180 degrees. Re-prime a second time to make sure fuel has passed through the injectors.

- Start the engine and operate at idle while engaging the marine gear to forward and reverse. This helps to circulate the oil prior to operation at sea.

- Once underway, check the engine periodically and have a great season. Don't forget the ever important *preventive* maintenance throughout the year.

DON'T LEAVE PORT WITHOUT...

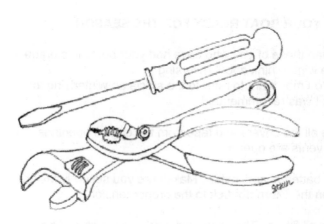

Let's talk about spare parts you should keep on your boat. Face it, storage space is very limited. The last thing you want to hear is someone offering advice as to what to fill the space with! However, having a few "extras" could mean the difference between making it to your destination or waiting for a benevolent soul or the Coast Guard to tow you in. This isn't as important for those of you who primarily take short day cruises, but for you adventurous ones who like to truly pick up stakes (or is that "cast off lines"?) and go 'splorin', it can be critical.

TOOLS. No book in the world is going to help you unless you have the proper tools to do the job. I posed this question to my service manager and one of my mechanics, and they recommended the following. All of these tools should fit into a small- to medium-size tool box.

- 3/8" Drive Socket Set
- 8" & 12" Crescent Wrench
- Needle Nose Pliers
- Vise Grips
- Assorted Screwdrivers
- Hammer
- Filter Wrench
- 3/8" - 3/4" Assortment of End Wrenches (box on one end, open on the other)
- Pry Bar (To assist in changing belts)

The parts you carry will be up to you. There are several "givens," such as spare BELTS, HOSES, and FILTERS. Carry EXTRA OIL, also.

Some additional extras you may want to have would be:
- a spare INJECTOR
- A THERMOSTAT
- GASKET, HOSE CLAMPS, FUEL PIPES (and necessary O-RINGS for installation)
- PUMP REPAIR KITS (BOTH WATER AND FUEL)

For an extended trip, take extra:
- INTAKE and EXHAUST VALVES
- VALVE SPRINGS
- VALVE SEALS
- VALVE KEEPERS (locks)
- an EXTRA INJECTOR
- a HEAD GASKET SET
- an EXTRA FUEL LIFT PUMP, if room permits
- HEAT EXCHANGER and OIL COOLER GASKETS

There are some products on the market that may also come in handy.
SILICON GASKET-MAKING MATERIAL is nice to have. This is available in

small tubes for easy storage. This can temporarily take the place of valve cover gaskets, oil pan gaskets, etc. It can also be applied to pre-cut gaskets to help the sealing process. A small tube of a thread-locking compound is valuable for bolts and screws that have a tendency to loosen. A small jar of naval jelly will help to remove rust.

There is at least one engine manufacturer that offers marine on-board repair kits. They are pre-packaged in a water-proof container. (I would bet it should be considered "water-resistant.") Ask you local dealer for availability and advice pertaining to your particular engine.

INSTRUMENTATION

Having good-quality instruments on your boat could help you avoid problems in the future, provided you are aware of what each of them is measuring. I would consider a tachometer, fuel level gauge, oil pressure gauge and temperature gauge to be the absolute minimum. We'll cover these first.

Let's begin with the TACHOMETER. This measures the revolutions per minute your engine is turning. Every manufacturer publishes a power curve (how much horsepower you should generate at a particular RPM rate). If you are aware of how fast you should be traveling at a particular engine RPM, you can easily monitor your engine performance. A noticeable variance means you are not getting maximum performance from your engine. This can be a valuable piece of information for your service technician in trouble-shooting your engine.

A FUEL LEVEL GAUGE is important for obvious reasons. You must know the capacity of your tank(s) and the gallons per hour your boat uses. Make sure your sending unit in your fuel tanks is mounted correctly to assure an accurate reading. The sender uses a float mechanism to measure the fuel. When the tank is full, it floats to the top. As the tank is emptied, the float stays at the top of the fuel, thus sending the level to the gauge.

The OIL PRESSURE GAUGE can also be helpful. Again, each engine is rated at a "normal" operating oil pressure. Know what your operating range is. If your pressure drops below the minimum, you do not have enough oil in your system to effectively and safely operate it. Without enough oil, you stand a good chance of blowing your engine and requiring a major overhaul or rebuild job. This can be very expensive compared to a little oil.

The last necessity is a TEMPERATURE GAUGE. If an engine overheats, the results can be anything from a simple blown head gasket to a cracked engine block. If the engine gets hot enough to crack the block, chances are you're looking at the expense of a new engine. Consult your operator's manual to determine the normal temperature for your engine. The sending unit for the gauge is usually mounted directly into the block (directly into a water-flow area) and acts very much like a household thermometer. Your engine could overheat for several reasons — such as a stuck thermostat, low coolant level, plugged heat exchanger, damaged sea water pump impeller, etc.

There are several instruments that are nice to have although not absolutely vital. One is an HOURMETER. Like an odometer in a car which tells you how many miles you have traveled, this tells you how many hours your engine (or generator) has run. Unlike a car in which you change your oil every three months or three thousand miles, usually your engine manufacturer recommends prescribed maintenance at certain hourly levels. Some tachometers have hourmeters built in.

Okay, now comes the fun part—electrics! I almost considered the ammeters and voltmeters as essential. You may want to consider them as such. An AMMETER is a device used to measure current. (By the way, an amp is 6,242,000,000,000,000,000 electrons flowing past a given point in one second.) An ammeter is connected in an electrical circuit in the same manner a flowmeter is connected to a fluid conductor. By monitoring your ammeter, you can determine whether you have enough current to run other electrical devices on your boat. This gauge would probably be considered more valuable for a generator engine than a propulsion engine. By computing the amperage needed for appliances, etc., you won't overload your generator.

A VOLTMETER measures voltage, which is electrical pressure. Unlike the location of an ammeter, a voltmeter is placed across the voltage source. For instance, a voltmeter would be placed in the wiring between a battery and an engine. 12-volt electrical systems are most common. Occasionally, you will find 24- and 32-volt systems in boats. If voltage falls too low, engine starting could be difficult and amperage would suffer, as well.

YOUR ENGINE'S CHRISTMAS WISH LIST

Dear Owner,

For years, I have given you tons of enjoyment (literally) and an avenue of *escape* from the rat race. I think I have been a good girl all those years, yet I am seldom remembered at Christmas. I am sending you my Christmas "Wish List" early because I know how busy you get this time of year. I really don't want much — just a few little things:

1   **OIL AND FILTER CHANGE.** This will help my overall attitude (and you KNOW I can quickly develop one!) It will keep me youthful and energetic.

2   **NEW BELTS AND HOSES.** Water and weather can be very corrosive to my rubber parts. I know you don't think I have a problem with my belts and hoses until they break. Sometimes, I can give you hints when this is about to happen, like frays in my belts and bumps in my hoses. However, when you usually notice, I'm always running. By getting me new ones each year, I'm less likely to leave you stranded.

3   **A GOOD CLEANING WITH DEGREASER.** By keeping me nice and clean, problem areas can be spotted with ease. Oil and fuel leaks will become obvious. (Be sure to read the cleaner's directions as some can damage my new belts and hoses.)

4   **PAINT TOUCH-UP.** After you've cleaned me, I know there will be a few areas that my paint is chipped or worn away. A quick spray with engine paint will keep me from rusting and corroding.

5   **A NEW IMPELLER FOR MY SEAWATER PUMP.** The rubber impeller in my raw water pump can deteriorate and get brittle. If small pieces break off, they can cause damage to my cooling system.

6   **A BATTERY CHECK-UP.** Inspect my terminals and cables. If you see any corrosion, you can use a wire brush to clean them. An ELECTROLYTE CHECK would also be nice. Look at my cables to make sure there are no cracks or worn spots.

7   **A FUEL/WATER SEPARATOR.** A lot of my friends have them and for good reason. Their owners know that this is a simple way to keep water out of my fuel system. The initial cost could seem a little high, but I know

116

you would rather spend a little now than to stand the cost of my overhaul or funeral later.

8   **ON-BOARD TOOL KIT.** You know the last time you needed a screwdriver and had to use a table knife? How about the time you needed a hammer and had to use the heel of your Topsiders? They didn't do too well, did they? A small tool kit with a flat-head screwdriver, a Phillips-head screwdriver, adjustable wrench and a hammer would be absolute minimum. I'll ask Becky to talk more about tools in a later article.

9   **SPARE PARTS KIT.** This wish is for my piece of mind, particularly on a cruise. Of course, the extent of this kit will depend on the extent of my tool kit. It's always a good idea to have extra belts, hoses and filters. In addition, an extra impeller for my raw water pump, a thermostat and gasket hose clamps could come in handy. For those of you who are mechanically inclined, extra injectors, valves, valve springs and a head gasket set are definite pluses. A tube of silicone can help make repairs easy. As always, WD-40 and duct tape are indispensable.

10 **Last, but not least, just a little TLC THROUGHOUT THE YEAR.** Remember, I'm only as good as the care I'm given.

Merry Christmas,
Your Engine

OVERHAUL OR NEW ENGINE?

No matter how well-cared for your engine is, there will come a time when an engine must either be overhauled or replaced.

If you own a larger, high-horsepower engine, replacement is going to the extreme, unless the engine has been totally fried. Depending on the size and make of the engine, a replacement could run upwards to $40,000. There are excellent rebuilt engines available for a quarter to half of this, also.

A complete overhaul should be a very extensive process. This will necessitate the removal of the engine from the boat. The engine block should be completely stripped of all components and thoroughly cleaned and tested for cracks. The crankshaft should be tested for cracks and alignment, and a micrometer should be used to verify that the shaft is up to specification.

Parts that should be replaced are the head(s), connective rods, pistons, liners, rings, main bearings, rod bearings, camshaft bearings, oil cooler core, thermostats, injectors, fuel jumper lines, all gaskets, hoses, belts and clamps. Major components such as water pumps, fuel pumps, fuel injection pumps, blowers, turbochargers, governors, etc. should be tested and replaced, if necessary. Many of these items are available rebuilt, which can save a lot of money.

After the major work is done, the engine should be started and checked for leaks and proper operating pressures and temperatures. If possible, the engine should be placed on a dynamometer and a load simulated. (If this is done, always ask for a copy of the print-out showing the results of the test.)

An in-frame overhaul could also be performed. This is done on the vessel and no extra shipyard expense for pulling the engine will be incurred. This overhaul is not as extensive as a complete overhaul, but everything previously mentioned is checked. Of course, the block and crankshaft cannot be cleaned and tested since the engine is remaining in the boat. If you have a smaller engine (similar to those in sailboats) you may opt for simply replacing the engine. Surprisingly, this can be actually less expensive than a major overhaul, especially when you consider that in order for any major work to be performed on one of these engines, it is necessary to remove the engine from the vessel. This can sometimes be a very good test of one's nerves. You should see how some engines we've worked on have been removed from sailboats. Creativity is a must!

GENERATORS (also known as "Gen Sets")

Not everyone has one, but, for those of you who do, there are some easy steps to take that will help you determine whether you have enough wattage to run all the appliances you want. Circuit breakers protect the generator set from an overload output. This occurs when too much load is applied at once, or if there is a short circuit in the system. To determine whether you will be able to run all the electrical appliances you want, you must make sure you know the maximum load that can be applied to your generator. Use the following formula to determine this (if you are unsure of the amount). Multiply the circuit breaker size by the AC output voltage. For example:

2 x 45 (amps) x 120 (volts) = 10800 watts, or

2 x 22.5 (amps) x 240 (volts) = 10800 watts

118

(These formulas are based on a 45 amp breaker on a 120V system.)

Check the wattage requirements of each appliance you wish to run at the same time. In most cases, the wattage can be found on the nameplate of the appliance. For example:

Air conditioner	1800 watts
Television	300 watts
Electric range (per element)	750 watts
TOTAL:	2850 watts

Remember, motorized appliances use more power during start-up than they do at normal speed. (Some motors draw as much as three times their operating power during start-up.) If you plan to use a motorized appliance, turn it on before starting other appliances. When the motor is running at normal speed, then you can start others.

If the circuit breaker trips, the genset will continue to run but will produce no electricity. If the breaker trips, turn off all appliances and reset the breaker. If it trips again, a short circuit is probable. (Call a mechanic at this point.) If it does not trip, turn on only as many appliances at the breaker size allows. If it trips again at this point, you may have a defective appliance or one without a proper ground.

If you have no need to run your generator, turn if off, or at least keep "no-load" operation to a minimum. With no load on the generator, combustion temperatures drop so low that fuel does not burn completely. This creates carbon deposits which clog injectors, glaze cylinders and cause piston rings and valves to stick. If it is necessary to run the engine for long periods, connect an electrical load to the generator output.

I'd like to add one last point of interest. Infrequent use can result in difficult starting and moisture condensation problems. This moisture is the result of the engine not being run long enough to reach normal operating temperature. In extreme cases, water may be deposited in the oil. If this happens, severe engine damage can result. To prevent this possibility, run the generator set under load at least one hour per week. Running for one long period each week is better than several short periods of operation. Remember, do not operate the set for long periods at no load.

YOUR BOAT'S LUBRICATION SYSTEM

Many of us take our engines for granted, whether it's in your boat, automobile, lawnmower (I put that in for those of us that dream of living aboard) or whatever, special attention and care must be given to the lubrication system.

The lubricating oil system consists of an oil pump, oil cooler, full flow oil filter(s), bypass valves at the oil cooler and filter(s), and pressure regulator valves at the lube oil pump and in the cylinder block main oil galley. I guess you can also include the oil pan.

The oil level in your engine should be checked daily with the engine stopped. (You should also check the oil level in your marine gear daily.) If necessary, add enough oil to raise the level to the proper mark on the dipstick. Remember, all diesel engines are designed to use some oil, so having to add oil occasionally is normal.

However, on the other side of the coin, if the oil level is constantly above normal, and you haven't added oil, contact a mechanic immediately. This could be an indication of fuel or coolant getting in the oil system and could cause serious damage to your engine.

Consult your owner's manual for oil change intervals. Detroit Diesel recommends that oil and oil filter be changed every 150 hours of engine operation. Remember to also use the weight of oil recommended by your engine manufacturer. By following these recommendations, the life of your engine will be extended.

Changing the oil on a boat is not as easy as on a truck or car. Boat owners seldom have room to remove the oil pan drain plug, place a receptacle underneath and dispose of the used oil. There are several inexpensive pumps that can be purchased to make this task easier. I've seen one that works as an attachment to an electric drill and another that connects directly to your battery. These work by feeding flexible tubing through the dipstick tube into the oil pan and pumping the oil up through the dipstick tube into a receptacle.

Please protect Mother Nature. Dispose of your used oil and filters in a responsible way. Make sure you take them to an authorized disposal outlet.

Carefully document the maintenance you perform (or have performed) for future use. These records will be valuable if you ever sell your boat or have to make a warranty claim.

QUESTIONS FROM WOMEN ABOARD

What is rolling? (Has to do with an engine having difficulty idling at low RPM's. Ours was due to water in the fuel line.)

Rolling is the uneven running, or a somewhat rhythmic surging, of the engine as a result of the injector rack sticking. In some cases, it is the result of a governor problem. It can also be the result of poor fuel. This Sea Sister was lucky in being able to identify the problem relatively easily.

Her second question has to do with the transport of fuel. *Is it true that all types of fuel are transported together (in the long container we sometimes see at the service station) separated by water?*

To get the answer to this question, I contacted one of our customers in the fuel transport business. It is true that all types of fuel can be transported together. However, in these cases, the fuels are in compartmentalized tanks, separated, not by water, but metal. It is true that oil and water do not mix, but attempting to separate fuel using water would cause extensive fuel contamination.

Around the Seattle area, due mostly to the Boeing influence, lubricity additives such as SuperLube are quite popular and for the more affluent, synthetic oils. With the lubricity additives the engines are said to run less hot, therefore retarding the breakdown of the oil. The synthetic oil is an expensive proposal initially, but supposedly it never needs to be changed or replaced. Are they really better for our engines? Is the cost justified? How much and how often should one add a lubricity additive? I'm curious about these options and would like to hear an expert's opinion on the subject. Perhaps others would be interested also.

Another Sea Sister adds: Someone we met in Lake Charles, LA, said that he adds a small amount of oil (such as 30W) to the diesel fuel in his tanks instead of using diesel additives. Will this accomplish the same thing and is it legal? A friend back in Port Aransas said that he had seen a system that would take old oil from the engines, place it in a reservoir and gradually feed

121

it to the fuel tanks as a method of recycling old oil. Have you heard of such a thing?

Okay — Let's start with the fuel. The "old style" diesel fuel had a high sulfur content which meant it was higher in lubricity (actually "oiled" parts of the fuel system.) With the reduction in sulfur content of the "new" fuel, this ability to "self-lubricate"(for lack of a better term) has been decreased. This has been blamed for problems in injection pumps and many other moving parts of the fuel system. There are several products on the market claiming to increase the lubricity of the fuel. Adding oil, in my opinion, would not be a viable solution, although it may work. Please bear in mind, these are FUEL additives, not oil additives.

Re: the question is about oil additives. Any quality oil will provide sufficient lubrication for an engine. There are many claims made by the manufacturers of synthetic oils. I have even heard one product claim that the SAE endorses it. That's well and good, but does YOUR engine manufacturer endorse the product and will oil-related failures be warrantable if the product is used? I represent three engine manufacturers and not one of them recommends the use of the super-duper, cure-all additives. As a matter of fact, one of my manufacturer's reps calls them *snake oils*. I suggest you follow the guidelines for maintenance set forth in your owner's manual. In my opinion, this is the safest way to go.

We have a 135 Ford Lehman and an 8 kw Westerbeke generator. The oil and filter is changed every 200 hours in the Lehman and every 100 hours in the Westerbeke, as per their service guides. We cruise the Lehman from 1800 to 2000 rpm. How many hours should we expect from these two engines before we have to have a major overhaul? As long as you are performing the prescribed maintenance, there is no reason why an engine shouldn't last a long, long time. How many hours is that?

Your guess is as good as mine. A good example of these is a Perkins we recently "rebuilt." This engine was a 1973 model with over 115,000 hours on it. There is no secret to this. Simply maintain the engine according to what the manufacturer recommends. We, in fact, had recommended that this gentleman NOT overhaul his engine. There was little to no wear on every part we examined. However, he was preparing to sail to Africa and wanted the insurance of a "new" engine. Chances are, 20 years from now, this engine still won't need an overhaul because of the immaculate care that has been given it. You are on the right track with your maintenance program. Keep it up!

A Sea Sister had a question about *varnishing in a gasoline engine.* Varnishing is a recent problem caused by the new oxygenated gasoline found in larger metropolitan areas of the country. The problems are usually in the carburetor. After being exposed to the air, this gasoline has a tendency to "varnish" or gel, leaving a shiny residue in the carburetor and causing the carburetor float to stick and "goo" to form, making the engine difficult to start. If there is no gas in the system, this can't happen.

What's the difference between 30W and 40W oil? Which one should I use?

The difference is the viscosity of the oil. What viscosity means can be confusing, so I'll attempt to explain a little further. The lower the "weight" of the oil, the thinner it is. Viscosity is affected by temperature. Think of it as watered-down Jell-O for a minute. While you are mixing it with hot water, it's runny and thin. When it cools, it thickens. When it is reheated, it becomes thin again. Now, back to oil.

Each manufacturer of engines does extensive research to determine the normal operating temperature of a particular engine and which weight oil would be the best to use. If the oil is too thin, as it is heated by the engine, it would break down too soon and become ineffective in controlling the friction. Too thick, it would not reach all the surfaces that needed to be coated.

I am going to give my stock answer as to which oil you should use — please consult your owner's manual. Most diesel manufacturers suggest you use a single weight oil, usually 30W or 40W. However, pay attention to the temperature ranges listed. If you live in an area that actually has a cold winter, your owner's manual may recommend you use a lighter weight oil in the winter so the air and water temperatures would not affect the viscosity as much. (Remember the Jell-O.) The reverse holds true in warmer weather.

Is it okay to use a multi-weight oil (10W40) in a diesel engine?

No. The multi-weight oils are not diesel approved. These are considered older specs for automobile engines. Every oil has an API (American Petroleum Institute) Service Classification assigned. The minimum diesel classification is CD, CE, or CG4. If a multi-weight oil has one of these API numbers, it can be used but is not recommended.

My source for the information on oil is Shell Oil Company. They have a group of three engineers who do nothing but answer questions. I told them what I needed and why, and boy! were they impressed with the idea of

WOMEN ABOARD!!! If you have any questions about oil, Shell's or any other brand, call them toll-free at 1-800-231-6950.

What does turbo-charged mean? Does a turbo-charged engine wear out faster than one that isn't?

Put very simply, when an engine is turbo-charged, more air is introduced into the combustion chamber via the turbo-charger. Combustion occurs when air is heated by compression to a temperature hot enough to ignite the diesel fuel, thus no spark is required. A turbo-charger uses heated air from the engine's own exhaust and re-introduces it into the combustion chamber. This pre-heated air is compressed by the piston just as it would be if it were "cooler" air, thus providing more power in the stroke.

A turbo-charged engine does not wear out any faster than a non-turbo'd engine. However, because exhaust air is being utilized, you must be careful to make sure your engine is performing efficiently (not smoking, etc.) Again, I cannot emphasize enough that wear on an engine is not so much a result of engine operation as it is a result of misuse and lack of maintenance.

Is it okay to use kerosene in a diesel engine?

Kerosene is actually #1 diesel fuel. Bear in mind that it does NOT contain the additives that the #2 fuel has. The sulfur content is different, as well. However, <u>IN AN EMERGENCY AND FOR A VERY LIMITED TIME</u>, kerosene can be used. Do not add any dead bacteria. Also, if it had been awhile since the engines were run and the Racor filters emptied, this could have been residual, settled gunk.

Don't assume that your tanks are clean because your fuel seems to be. There may be sediment at the bottom of them. I don't know the procedure for checking, but a local shipyard should be able to do it easily. Then make the decision to clean the tanks or not.

Another Sea Sister owns a 1978 Ocean Winds catamaran sailboat. It's powered by two 15 horsepower Yanmar diesel engines. The port engine has 1232 hours on it while the starboard has 1072. She's concerned about the life expectancy of these engines. She's also cleaning the bilge and engines and wonders what paint to use to paint the engines.

There is no pat answer as to how long a life you can expect from your engines. The amount of life in an engine depends on the care and

124

maintenance it has been given. Has the preventive maintenance been performed according to the manufacturer's recommendations? Have either of the engines had any major work done to them and, if so, what was done? Remember, if properly maintained, an engine will give many, many years of service. (By the way, ask any of the Sea Sisters about how I preach maintenance. It's a continuous process, but worth the effort.)

The painting solution should be much easier. If, after cleaning an engine, there are a few spots that need a touch-up, simply go to your local engine dealer and ask for a spray can of engine paint. A good dealer will have no less than two options. You can buy paint that has the engine brand name (in this case, Yanmar) on it and pay an exorbitant amount of money for it. Or, you can purchase a good brand (i.e. Krylon) of engine paint for (at the very least) half the price. Sometimes, the color will be close enough that you will have to hunt to find where your touch-up was made to see the difference. A good example is Detroit Diesel paint. A 12-ounce spray can runs $10.22. I sell the exact same color in Krylon for $3.75. Try to specify engine paint as it is designed to withstand heat, etc. that will normally occur. Remember to always keep bare metal surfaces painted, especially in salt-air environments. You'll be grateful later.

I've learned through the grapevine that part of my last article has been discussed in several pubs. The topic under discussion is the use of kerosene as fuel in diesel engines. Someone asked, *What is the difference between #1 and #2 diesel fuel and since home-heating oil is basically kerosene, why can't this be used as fuel?*

I am having a difficult time finding the differences in #1 and #2 fuel. I have a fuel specification chart which is chock-full of numbers that, quite frankly, are Greek to me. The information I have concerns fuel that is approved for Detroit Diesel engines. The flash point of #1 fuel is lower than #2 which could lead to improper combustion. However, the bulletin also states that when prolonged idling periods or cold weather conditions below freezing are encountered, the use of 1-D fuel is recommended. (Remember, this is Detroit Diesel speaking and not Cummins, Cat, etc.) Always consult the manufacturer of your engine for more information.

The bulletin has three paragraphs about alternative fuels, including fuels marketed as premium diesel fuels and kerosene-based jet fuels. Because these types and "winter-blended" diesel fuels have a lower volumnmetric heat content than the standard 2-D fuel, operating with these fuels will result in reduced engine performance (as much as 5% in output and mileage).

125

These fuels are also lower in viscosity than 2-D fuel, therefore, a filtration system recommended for "severe duty service" should be changed to prevent potential injector seizure from dirt contamination.

I won't say it's okay to burn these fuels on a full-time basis. I will say that in an emergency, and for limited periods of time, you should not cause any damage to your engine if you do. I'm going to continue to research this topic. I have a strong feeling that the can of worms is not open, it's just ajar!

I've seen some filter funnels at the marine stores for filtering dirt and water when you fuel up. Do they work?

Yes, to a degree. They will take out the big chunks. A good fuel filter, in conjunction with fuel treatment, will do a much better job at filtering and dispersing water. If you have a consistent water problem in your fuel, a fuel/water separator works very well.

The next questions are about batteries. *What is the difference between wet and gel batteries? Which is better? What is a deep cycle battery?*

A wet battery is one that contains the standard liquid electrolyte that we're all familiar with. A gel battery contains a gel substance instead. The gel batteries were designed for use in applications in which a possibility of the battery turning over is of concern. A good example of this is motorized wheelchairs.
A deep-cycle battery is one that is designed to be used for extended periods of time. The key word here is USED. Deep cycle batteries are like the ones used on cordless phones. They must be charged, then used until the power is virtually gone, then recharged. If they are not used in this manner, a "memory" is developed. For instance, if you place the battery on a charger before the power is depleted, the battery then "thinks" that this is as low as the power level should become and you will not get as much time from the second (and any future) charges.

What are risers and how often should I replace them?

Depending on your terminology, risers can be one of two things. They are an integral part of a boat's exhaust system or they are part of your engine. The exhaust risers are exhaust tubes with an upward bend in them, something sort of like an upside-down U. This bend is in the exhaust piping to prevent water from entering the engine through the exhaust which can cause engine damage. How often they are changed depends on the shape they are in.

They normally do not need "periodic" replacement, only periodic inspection. Check for leaks and deterioration. *Please wait until they've cooled before touching.* Engine risers are also called *lifters* or *cam followers.* These are the little doo-dads that ride on the cam shaft and help to work the valves. They should be inspected and replaced as necessary with every engine overhaul.

Someone was telling me about a new model Caterpillar engine that it's okay to pour your used motor oil into the fuel tank and burn it along with the fuel. Ever heard of such a thing? Can I do that to our Perkins 6.354T's?

Although I'm not a Cat dealer, I called the Caterpillar distributor in Houston for the answer to this one. The answer is NO, NO NO. Many years ago, Cat made an engine that they claimed would run with some used oil in the fuel. They no longer say this. Putting used motor oil into your fuel can cause very extensive damage to your fuel system. Imagine all the dirty particles from your old engine oil trying to get through an injector tip. Granted, fuel filters will catch the larger pieces, but I can guarantee they won't catch them all. If you get a wild hair and decide to try this, please make sure you are in the Galveston area so I can do the major overhaul you are sure to need! We could use the business!

What additives do you recommend in the fuel tank, if any? On our ICW trip two years ago we had major 'dirty' fuel problems. Are there different additives for different climates? Do you recommend the use of a separate filter at the fill opening on the boat itself? We have a sailboat with diesel auxiliary and many friends now use a Baja filter. We found this slowed the process considerably. The spout of the filter didn't fit well into the fill opening, causing great difficulty. After many cleanings and fuel filterings, we replaced the fuel tank with one that now has opening ports so we can reach in and clean, if necessary. We use Biobor each time we fill up and never buy fuel from a dock that doesn't have filters right on the pumps. We also never buy fuel from locations that don't pump a lot of fuel year round. Are we being overly cautious and are we doing the right things?

A good diesel fuel conditioner like FPPF or Megatane should be sufficient. Both products disperse water and aid in fuel efficiency. This makes for cleaner and more complete fuel burn which translates into slightly less gallons per hour of fuel burned. There are some additional additives that are used in very cold climates. These are used to aid in cold-starting situations. There are several on the market. They aid in cold starts by preventing paraffin gelling. Check the label on the product to verify the temperature ranges in which they are most effective.

As far as a pre-filtering system goes, it usually is not necessary. If filters are on the pumps, most of the "big stuff" is being caught. A fill-opening filter may catch a little more, but it may be insignificant. An initially expensive, but in the long run relatively inexpensive, system to use is a fuel/water separator as a primary filter with your normal fuel filter(s) on your engine. This filter will separate any water and residual gunk before it goes to your engine fuel filters. The engine filters can catch whatever may be left. The Racor fuel-water separator is probably the best known and the replacement elements come in 2, 10, or 30 micron ratings. Use common sense in selecting the elements. If you know you've taken on some bad fuel, start with the 2 micron until the next fill up. This element will get restricted much faster than the 10 or 30, which means it must be replaced more often. It's also a good idea to use the 2 micron after you've used a biocide. The dead algae and bacteria will be trapped before entering your system. On refueling with good fuel, you probably would want to change to the 10 or 30 micron, which should be more than adequate for decent fuel.

I'm not familiar with Biobor. From the sound of the name, it sounds like a biocide. If you have *chronic* algae problems, using it on each fill up may be necessary. Most folks would be better off using a fuel conditioner with each fill-up and only using a biocide as needed.

Any caution you use to protect your engine is commendable. Remember to always follow the engine manufacturer's recommendations for prescribed maintenance and you'll be fine.

Would you educate us on the colors of diesel smoke? What does the color tell you about how the engines are running? Does temperature or humidity have any influence as with gas engines?

From what I've been told, this varies from manufacturer to manufacturer. For instance, a two-cycle engine producing black smoke may have an entirely different reason for it than a four-cycle engine. So, here we are back to my "stock answer." Refer to the trouble-shooting section of the service manual for your particular engine. This probably isn't what you wanted to hear, but I don't have access to all the service manuals necessary to accurately answer this question.

128

We put a new Westerbeke 42B in old Sea Yawl last September under very adverse conditions. It has never gotten over 1 gallon/hour during its 360 hours aboard. For the last two fill-ups it is down to almost 1.5 gallon/hour. Help! What can we do? We are heading south on the ICW so the motor is not under any undue strain as in beating against waves. The Westerbeke that collapsed last year in Lake Huron with only 100 hours consistently got .5 gallons/hour which is what the manual indicates is normal. Any advice you have will be appreciated!!

According to my informed sources, there may be an excessive load on the engine. This could be caused by several things. It may not be the engine itself.

You did not elaborate as to what the "adverse conditions" were under which you replaced the last engine. This could have some bearing as to what might be the cause of the high fuel consumption.

The bearings on your output shaft may have been damaged. A bent prop shaft or incorrectly sized prop could be the culprit. With the marine gear in neutral, take a small wrench (10" or so should do it), tighten it around the output shaft and try to manually turn the shaft. If it doesn't turn fairly easily, it could be bent or have bad bearings. It would also be a good idea to have the marine gear checked. There may be a problem there that could cause the fuel consumption.

If your engine "locked up," you could have bent the shaft. Did you replace a 42B with a 42B? Look in your owner's manual or service manual's troubleshooting section under High Fuel Use and see what that says. (My guess is the service manual will provide a few more details than the owner/operator manual.) Specific problems like this are always a shot in the dark. It's so much easier to address generalities, but we try!

ENGINE ROOM TIPS FROM *WOMEN ABOARD*

- We keep one light on in the engine room at all times. If there's an emergency there, we don't want to be groping around for the light switch.

- Spare parts and plenty of tools are necessities.

- Think about having a few pieces of flat rubber stored under a bunk mattress. They act as a temporary patch, or a replacement for a seal, washer or gasket. They can be purchased in 6-12" wide by 3-4' long sheets with various thickness'.

- Engine zincs are unique to particular boats, and not always available in small ports. Carry ones set up with brass plugs.

- Two empty 5-gallon cans (for waste oil), extra belts, and far more fuel filters than you think you need (especially if you take on bad fuel) will not set you back financially, but will be a godsend if occasion calls.

- Handy products to have on hand include liquid electrical tape to seal connections against corrosion and 3M™ SUPER WEATHERSTRIP ADHESIVE to bond rubber to metal in areas of high stress.

- GUNK® General Purpose Degreaser in liquid form (cheaper than aerosol) cleans diesel engines. Use an all-purpose sprayer to apply.

- TEF-GEL® stops corrosion where a stainless steel bolt comes in contact with aluminum.

- Try LOCTITE® Removable Thread Locker for any nut/bolt assembly that might vibrate loose.

- STAR BRITE® SNAP & ZIPPER LUBRICANT protects against jamming and binding caused by salt. Epoxy putty sticks, regular and metal, work for difficult repairs to fiberglass, metal and wood—and can be used underwater.

- Kitty litter puts out fires or absorbs engine room oil. And duct tape will fix anything. It always sticks.

- You've seen it in the cartoons to stop sudden leaks, but don't rule out the simple things. A wooden cork sized for each thru-hull fitting can be attached to same with a light string. Any marine store or catalog sells them in sets of four graduated sizes.

- Don't forget to carry extra breakers. If a faulty one causes your air conditioner to go out in the tropics, you'll give thanks.

130

- Under "expensive spare parts," consider an extra propeller, or even two. If you ding one, in some areas you will have to fly in a diver, fly the damaged prop out for repair and back again to reinstall. The "extras" suddenly became cheaper.

- Besides the well-stocked tool chest, a full kit of adapters tops the list. Double 30's into a single 50 amp outlet, single 30 amp to a single 15 amp, etc.

- Cordless battery-operated tools, such as a screwdriver or drill (with chargers), come in handy.

- A Sea Sister on the Great Lakes carries a hacksaw blade. A stray line, wrapped around their prop, disappears in fine order. And water goggles allow a clear look at the offending mess.

- One boater won't leave without her Leatherman®, an all-in-one tool that includes knife, pliers, screwdrivers, scissors, wire cutters, and more. Another captain requires those on board to carry a pocketknife at all times. In an emergency, you don't want to be looking for one.

- A Dremel® tool (and small inverter if needed) has many uses. With the huge range of bits for cutting, grinding, drilling, and polishing, this is a wonderful boat addition, complete with low power draw.

- A low-amp anchor light with solar sensor may serve your purposes. At 0.1-0.2 amps, you can leave it plugged in and to ashore at noon without worrying about wasted amps or no light after sundown.

- Halogen lights aid in any night emergency. Don't forget waterproof flashlights of various sizes (with extra batteries) and consider a 12VDC plug-in type with a long cord.

- Hella® fans run all day without draining your batteries when the wind doesn't blow and the sun does shine. They draw around 200mA. All kinds of fans help in warm climates, including 12V, handheld, and battery operated.

131

CRUISING WITH *WOMEN ABOARD*

George Town (Exuma, Bahamas) has been the site of weekly get-togethers of *WOMEN ABOARD* for several years. In February 1998, all cruising women were invited to the discussion with 27 attending. Small groups discussed boating "from a woman's point of view," and there was so much interplay that the group decided to continue the discussion the following week.

Twenty-nine women met on February 12 at the St. Andrew's Anglican Church Community Center in George Town. Their "homework" was to bring a list of the 10 THINGS YOU WOULDN'T LEAVE THE DOCK WITHOUT. The results were tabulated and presented on February 20th at a luncheon at Eddie's Edgewater Restaurant with 46 women attending!

The homework resulted in some very interesting responses. You just might be interested to know what they wouldn't leave the dock without! These are the most frequently listed items:

10 THINGS I WOULDN'T LEAVE THE DOCK WITHOUT

1. Partner (listed as husband, captain, first mate, skipper, my licensed marine engineer, baby-sitter/co-parent)
2. Books (novels, yoga, medication, Bible, atlas, dictionary, hymnal, devotional books, cookbooks)
3. Watermaker

132

4. Intangibles (patience, fewer things, prayer, knowledge of bread-making, good way to do laundry, positive attitude, tolerance, smile, sense of humor)
5. GPS (Global Positioning System)
6. SSB (Single-sideband Radio)
7. Credit cards/money
8. Plastic bags
9. Dinghy (good and big)
10. Drinks (beer, wine, soda, alcohol, tea, Crystal Light, juices)

OTHER ITEMS (Categorized, but not in any specific order)

<u>Pets</u> (dog and cat)

<u>Communications and Reminders of Home</u>
- Family photos (children/grandchildren/family)
- Stationary/greeting cards/stamps/address book
- Phone cards
- Good mail service or e-mail

<u>Boat Equipment</u>
- Side curtains/dodger/bimini
- Compass
- Autopilot
- Good and big anchor and chain
- Saltwater pump
- Spare parts
- Well-found or bigger boat
- Inverter
- Siphon tubes/equipment
- Solar panels
- Jack lines/harnesses
- Lots of propane gas
- Bug screens
- VHF
- Depth sounder
- Lots of fuel
- Sunshower
- Foul weather gear
- Charts

- Head repair kit
- Wind generator
- Binoculars
- Windless
- Refrigerator/freezer

Dinghy Equipment
- Good dinghy with big outboard (15+ hp)
- Safety gear

Recreation
- Books (see Top 10 list)
- Computer/printer
- Word processor
- Cassettes
- Radio
- CD player/CDs
- Calculator
- Camera and film
- Art supplies (watercolors, sketch pad, pencils, calligraphy pens, ink)
- Arts and crafts projects
- More distractions for the crew
- Crossword puzzles
- Jigsaw puzzles
- Playing cards
- TV/VCR/videos
- Keyboard; music
- Fishing gear
- Aerobic tapes
- Walkman
- Snorkeling gear
- View bucket
- Games

Provisions
- Drinks (see Top 10 list)
- Lots of food
- Paper products
- Snacks (popcorn)
- Water

- Green vegetable bags for storage
- Plastic bags
- Canned goods (mushrooms, meat)
- Green tea
- Hard candy
- Recipes
- Toddy coffee
- Sproud seeds
- Powdered milk
- Sweet pickles
- Curry paste
- Thai ingredients
- Peanut butter
- Bread/biscuit mixes
- Sushi ingredients
- Bay leaves

Medical
- Prescription medicine
- Hormone pills
- Eye glasses/contacts/extras
- Seasick remedies (candy ginger, wrist cuffs, Marezine)
- First aid kit
- Q-tips
- Toothpicks
- Vaseline
- Gamma globulin shot
- Vitamins
- Merk manual
- Herbal stress reliever
- Instant-read thermometer
- Kids Tylenol
- Antacid tablets
- Hydrocortisone cream

Household Items
- Collapsible crates
- Thermos
- China/dishes/real glasses
- Water jugs with spigots

- Plastic jar for garbage
- Duct tape
- WD 40/Bioshield
- Bug repellent/citronella candles
- Pressure cooker
- Cutting board
- Special pillows/down pillows
- Water filters
- Down comforter
- Can opener
- Force 10 oven
- Bucket on deck for rinsing sand off shoes
- Mirrors, assorted sizes
- Knives (variety)
- Salad spinner
- Tupperware
- Candles
- Tools
- Potpourri
- Coffee grinder
- Coffee maker
- Cold drink holders
- Corkscrew
- Pots/pans

The years of respondent experience added up to show the real needs: Three of the most important things to take from the dock are a *sense of humor, plenty of time*, and *a boundless sense of adventure.*

Bring with you a game plan to anticipate the worst case scenario, and hope for the best. Tempers can flare with high winds and heavy seas, but don't forget your purpose for being there in the first place.

TIPS ON BEING PREPARED FOR A
COAST GUARD BOARDING

Have you ever worried about being boarded by the Coast Guard? Occasionally that spector has flitted through my mind, chased by other, more pressing cruiser's worries: Will the anchor hold? What's leaking *now*? Do we have enough food/spare parts/toilet paper?

Aboard *Mañana,* we have always tried to be in compliance with all state and federal requirements, both for our own safety, and because we had seen others boarded. One night I awoke from a particularly bad dream with a vivid mental picture of our important ship's papers, surrounded, as they in fact were, by news stories, questionable cartoons, and other items not calculated to inspire the sympathies of a Coast Guard Boarding Officer.

That very day I went out and bought a new, clean notebook, labeled it "Ship's Papers" and started over. With a large supply of plastic page protectors, I tried to organize what I thought they'd want to see. I used the pamphlet "Federal Requirements and Safety Tips for Recreational Boats" as my outline. It is available from any Coast Guard or Auxiliary office (and frequently from state licensing offices, or call 1-800-368-5647, the USCG Boating Safety Hotline, as well as West Marine, Boat/U.S., etc.)

Item #1 in our notebook is our original documentation paper. Item #2 is our Radio Station License (yes, they're supposed to be displayed by the radio, but, unless you have a nav station or pilot house, I wouldn't consider it a real decorating asset.) Item #3, because we are "40 ft. or longer," is our WRITTEN "Waste Management Plan." It says that we will throw waste only in the trash can, and Tom will take the contents of the trash can ashore for disposal. Item #4, in case they missed the decal outside the boat, is our courtesy exam paper from the Auxiliary. Behind that I added the booklet I had used to compile this info, a booklet of our state requirements, and just because it seemed the logical place for me to file it, all the information I have accumulated from Boat/U.S. about salvage and tow services.

With three boarding experiences under our belts (once on a delivery trip, with the owner on board, and twice on our own boats—December '95 on the old *Mañana,* and March '96 on the new one—I can describe what has happened to us, as all three experiences have been remarkably similar.

After the radio hail comes the big question, *When were you last boarded?* The next two are anticlimactic: *How many people do you have on board?* and *"Do you have a weapon?"* Then the instructions: "Maintain course and reduce speed so that we can come along side." By this time I'm scurrying for our Ship's Papers notebook and drivers' licenses. By the time I have all three items on the bridge they are nearly alongside. By all means, summon a smile, extend a hand, and welcome them aboard. (Remember, they're nervous, too!)

They'll ask if this is everyone on board, for some form of identification (they're probably on the lookout for people previously associated with piracy, theft or the like) and WHERE IS THE WEAPON? Try NOT to do as I once did—hurry away to get it, then turn and hand it to the officer. He nearly fainted, and I nearly started crying. (We carry a long-barreled shotgun, selected because it is usually seen as a defensive, rather than offensive, weapon.) The officer would much rather you *tell* him where it is and offer to lead him/her to it. They will look for shells in the chamber and copy down the serial number. This last time Tom asked how they feel about finding cruisers with guns. The reply was that they were more concerned when they got a *negative* answer.

These two topics taken care of, the whole boarding party visibly relaxes. If you have, at least in your own mind, maintained the fiction that this is just a friendly visit until this point, you've got it made. All three experiences, coincidentally, have occurred on Tom's watch. He just steered and allowed me to be spokesperson. I tried to limit my conversation to answering questions. (Those of you who know me know how difficult *that* was.) I figured that volunteering anything extra, or out of order, would not speed things up, and just might get me in trouble.

They wanted to see life jackets (and checked them for signs of aging/abuse by squeezing and twisting), flares (checked for dates), fire extinguishers and a 'sound producing' device. They looked around the head for a Y-valve/overboard discharge, in the engine room for the placard for oil discharge, the holding tank, and wanted to see a through-hull wire tied shut. (Because we were underway and the outlet hose led between the running engine and the generator, he gave up on that search. Can't say I blame him.)

He also asked me if I had a garbage placard in the galley (I do, inside the cabinet directly over the garbage can, very visible when the cabinet door is open. He seemed satisfied with that.) The very last item he asked for was a copy of the Nav. Rules of the Road. We just happened to have an old copy aboard. He accepted it, but mentioned that a *few* changes have been made since 1976, and that we might possibly want to get a new one.

138

Checklist complete, the Boarding Report was signed by the Boarding Officer and a copy given to us. They also pointed out the information verifying this boarding, should another Coast Guard vessel ask that loaded question, *When were you last boarded?* After a few pleasantries about our boat, the weather, and our cruise, they packed up and left. Each visit lasted less than 45 minutes, although at the time it seemed much longer. We were allowed to continue on our way, at normal speed, except while they were getting on and off. They were polite, businesslike, and the whole experience was relatively painless. A Coast Guard boarding is nothing to be afraid of, but it IS an experience that should be anticipated and planned for.

- Original Documentation paper

- Radio Station License, required for U.S. vessels leaving the country, or anyone operating single-sideband radio. No radio license is required for VHF radios, EPIRBs, radar, GPS, Loran, CB or amateur radio (an amateur license is required.)

- *Written* "Waste Management Plan" (if 40 ft. or longer)

- Courtesy Exam paper (if received from the Coast Guard Auxiliary)

- Driver's licenses (or some form of identification for those on board)

- If you have weapons on board (and you <u>will be asked</u> if you do), tell the boarding officer where it is and if she would like you to lead her to it. The serial number will be copied down and whether or not there are shells in the chamber will be noted.

- Life jackets (They will be checked for signs of aging/abuse by squeezing and twisting)

- Flares (Checked for dates)

- Fire extinguishers

- A "sound producing" device

- The head will be checked for a Y-valve/overboard discharge, the engine room for the placard for oil discharge, the holding tank, and whether or not the thru-hull is wire-tied shut.

- Garbage placard in the galley

- Navigation Rules of the Road (make sure you have a copy if your boat is 40 feet or more.)

SPECIAL INFO FOR THE GULF INTRACOASTAL WATERWAY (GICW)

When cruising the ICW, particularly in Louisiana, plan your overnight stops carefully, ahead of time. There are lots of miles along that narrow stretch of the waterway with no marinas and no safe places to anchor. Don't assume the many canals you'll see off the side of the bayous are safe. Many are now barricaded off, and many of the rest of them are still used by the oil and tow boat companies. You certainly don't want to wake up in the middle of the night to find a tow pushing a barge right beside your bunk. Local knowledge is truly a life saver and the locals, approached politely, will usually be more than happy to share that knowledge.

Because large ships and commercial tow boats with barges truly CANNOT stop for you, and because sometimes they *really do* need to take their half out of the middle of the channel, anytime you're in a narrow waterway or near a bend in the channel, you MUST be aware of their locations and what they intend to do. Listen carefully to them on the VHF (I've listed some of the channels at he end of this paragraph.) You'll hear them state their location, their direction of travel, and sometimes what they're carrying. You must pay close attention to where YOU are along the waterway all the time. (I use a clothes pin along the edge of our big chart book, moving it along as I confirm passing the rare buoys or any other useable landmark.)

If you hear a tow within a couple of miles, respond on the radio mentioning your location with reference to ICW mile markers, and your direction of travel. They may not answer, but they ARE listening. You can't go wrong singing out your location! If they respond to you, CO-OPERATE!

Remember the Big Boat Rule: BIG BOATS GO FIRST! And try to remind yourself that they're out here earning their living. We're out here, presumably, to have fun. All the rules favor them and for a very good economic reason. Remember, they're PUSHING their loads and so may maneuver in ways that seem very odd to us. One of the guidebooks suggests you try to PUSH a foot ruler around on a table top to get a feel for what they have to do with their boats to make the head of that first barge move in the desired direction. Also, be alert for tows pushing empty

140

barges—these are the most difficult for them to maintain control of, especially in any type of cross wind!

Monitor Channel 13 through all of Louisiana and on to the western edge of Houston's Ship Channel. Channel 16 for most of the rest of the Gulf ICW except Morgan City, where the MANDATORY (that means all of us!) Berwick Vessel Traffic Control is on VHF Channel 11. Up the Tenn-Tom the tows use Channel 16, but on the Tennessee River we didn't hear them talking, so we asked a passing tow, on 16 (they are supposed to monitor both) what the commercial boats were using, and discovered it was 13 there.

Be alert in the New Orleans locks, particularly the Industrial Lock. It is very old and its sheer walls offer nothing for you to tie up to, so they have to drop a messenger line down to you. You must have already rigged your own dock lines (20 to 25 ft. minimum) to your bow (or front spring cleat) and stern. Tie big loops in the end (they have to slip over large bollards), and bring both loops to the same location on deck. When the line handler drops his line to you, be ready to tie your loops to it. That way, even if he puts both loops over the same bollard, you have a line bow and stern, giving you some control. (They're better now, but in the past, on more than one occasion, they've failed to take a second line. When the inevitable tow boat in front of us put his engines into gear our single screw vessel was no longer under our control. NOT a comfortable feeling!)

TOWBOATS AND RADIOS
from *Texas Mariner*

Many of the Texas Mariner Cruisers Association (TMCA) cruises takes us into Bolivar Roads and the ICW. Consequently, we pleasure sailors come into close contact with a lot of commercial towboat traffic. One fact has impressed me greatly since I learned it at a past TMCA meeting: towboats require about one mile to stop! Several things can greatly enhance the safety of our encounters with towboats and also improve the interaction between pleasure boaters and working towboats. One of the most important things is your VHF radio. Learn to use it properly and then USE IT! Below are some suggested guidelines:

• Know where you are on the ICW within the nearest mile. This means paying attention to the mile markers (those blue and white signs every five statute miles) and your charts. There are a lot of towboats and

141

pleasure boats on the ICW, so it doesn't do much good to identify yourself as the "eastbound sailboat on Matagorda Bay."

- There are two directions on the Texas ICW: eastbound toward New Orleans and westbound toward Port Isabel.

- When a towboat is visible and about two miles away (two boats approaching at 5 knots each will cover one statute mile in about 5½ minutes), contact the captain on the hailing channel (13 or 16, see below). Say "This is the eastbound sailboat *Cambria* approaching the westbound towboat at about mile marker 525. Which side would you like me to pass?" The towboat captain will almost always answer. In case he does not, repeat your request. If he still does not answer, say "This is the eastbound sailboat *Cambria* near mile marker 525 approaching the westbound towboat. We intend to pass on the one (or two) whistle." Once the towboat has given you the desired side to pass, confirm it by saying "This is the sailboat *Cambria*. We will pass on the one (or two, whichever he designated) whistle. Thank you and have a good day, Captain."

- One whistle means that you will alter course to starboard to pass, so that you and approaching boat will pass port side to port side. Two whistles means that you will alter course to port, so that you will pass starboard side to starboard side. Whistle terminology is from the former use of whistle signals instead of VHF radios to signal passing intentions.

- The same procedure should be used when overtaking and passing a towboat. Contact the towboat as you come up astern. Since you can probably read the name, say "This is the eastbound sailboat approaching astern of the towboat *Brown Bear*. We would like to pass, captain. What side would you like us on?" The towboat captain may be able to see ahead better than you and he may advise of oncoming traffic or a navigational hazard. When the captain advises on the passing side, confirm it with a response similar to item discussed previously.

- When approaching a bend in the ICW, a bridge, or a lock which obscures your visibility ahead, it is a good practice to say on the hailing channel (16 or 13), "This is the westbound sailboat *Cambria* approaching the bend on the ICW at about mile marker 440, checking for any concerned eastbound traffic."

- Towboats monitor Channel 13 east of Pelican Cut and on the Houston Ship Channel, and Channel 16 to the west of Pelican Cut. If you fail to get an answer on one of these channels, switch to the other and try again.

- Bridges and locks monitor Channel 13, except the Galveston Causeway Bridge (who likes to talk on Channel 10.) They need to be contacted as you approach them. Say "This is the westbound sailboat approaching the east Brazos River floodgate requesting permission to pass through." Wait for the lock/floodgate/bridge tender to respond and give you instructions.

- If you are unsure of what a towboat is doing (aground, maneuvering into a lock, entering from another channel, etc.), contact them on the VHF and discuss the situation.

PACKING FOR AN OFF-SHORE DELIVERY

What does one take when making a delivery of a boat across an ocean? The answer lies in the questions one must ask about the boat and about the passage.

The first thing to consider is the type of boat and the amenities available during the crossing. Some boats are well equipped with everything on board except your personal items, while others are sparsely outfitted, requiring you to bring items such as your own towels, pillow, bedding and personal floatation devices. Ask so you know where your boat fits into the scheme of things.

What you bring is also greatly determined by the climate you will be sailing in—all tropical, all temperate, or crossing from one to the other.

The length of the trip, if it includes an offshore passage, does not usually change what you bring, just how much you bring of each item.

The following is a list of what one Sea Sister packed for a 6-week journey, including a four-week ocean passage. It can also be adapted for shorter coastal cruises. Use it as a starting point and adjust according for your own situation.

CLOTHES

Consider bringing three of just about everything—one on, one dirty, one drying.

Natural fibers, i.e. cotton, takes so long to dry especially if the material is very heavy and salt-laden. This Sea Sister bought a top and pants set of "Quick Dry" material, made of a special nylon material, made with plenty of venting for air circulation. They were great for protection from the sun but cooler than any other clothes, yet at the same time kept her warm on night watches. They dry almost instantly whether the water is from rain, spray or washing. You can even get long pants that turn into shorts by unzipping the legs. Remember, everything on a boat needs to have more than one use!

Shirts
Loose fitting shirts are great as a cover-up over bathing suits, protection of sensitive areas from the sun, and for warmth before you need a sweater.

Shirts are much cooler than T-shirts and usually take a shorter time to dry.

Tank tops
Worn more often when closer to the equator and when it got hot below decks due to closing the hatches in rain or heavy seas.

T-shirts
Loose fitting was best to allow air circulation when hot.

Long Pants

Shorts

Outerwear
Fleece cardigan, lightweight rain jacket, sweatshirt.

Socks
In temperate climates, regular and thick wool socks would be a must.

Underwear

Bathing suits
Two, preferably with different coverage areas

144

Hats
The "Head Gasket", made of neoprene with Velcro closure, is   available from West Marine. I also brought a hard visor for when the wind was so strong it made the neoprene useless. Pin a glasses keeper to the hat and to your top to prevent losing your head gear in the wind.

Sunglasses
Consider those that give good UV protection; that wraps around to block out glare; that allows air to flow and fit over reading glasses.

PERSONAL

Shampoo
If water conservation will be an issue make sure your shampoo will lather in salt water—some will, some won't.

Soap
If water conservation will be an issue you may need salt-water soap in addition to your regular soap. (Regular soap WILL NOT later in salt water. In fact it turns hard and is difficult to rinse off.) An alternative to salt-water soap that many boaters use is Joy or Palmolive dish soap—works great, is easily available, is much more economical, and has more than one use on a boat!

Skin Cleanser
An alternative to using soap and water on your face and a good way to get off the sun block is a good non-alcohol based skin cleanser. Remember to take cotton pads to apply the cleanser.

Lotion
Hand and body lotion helps with peeling skin, which it invariably does when around so much sun and salt.

Sun Block
Bring plenty of it.   Remember to take protection for your lips as well. Zinc Stick goes on like lipstick and comes in many different colors, as well as white.

Vitamins
Especially important on long passages when fresh fruits and vegetables will not be available.

Travel mask
For sleeping during the day after completing a night watch.

Earplugs
Bring several pairs, and store them in a snack-size Ziploc bag.

Diary
Get into the habit of recording your daily activities. You will be amazed how they all run into one after some time at sea.

Time Pieces
Make sure that yours is water resistant and that that it very easy to see even on the darkest night. An alarm is nice to have too.

Miscellaneous
Remember all the regular toiletries you would use at home (toothpaste, toothbrush, dental floss, deodorant, Q-tips, razor and blades, travel-size shaving cream, etc.) Remember towels if they won't be available on the boat.

BOATING GEAR

PFD
Although most boats have PFD's available, you might want to bring you own if you want to make sure you're comfortable. Mustang, West Marine and a few other manufacturers make inflatable horseshoe-type PFD's that either self-inflate upon impact with the water or can (or must) be manually inflated with a CO_2 cartridge or with a mouth piece. These also usually have a built-in safety harness. Before you purchase this type be sure you can comfortably wear it.

Rain boots
We brought our dive booties (with rubber soles), though rain boots would be necessary in temperate climates.

Rain gear
A lightweight jacket and pants are a must for the tropics. They provide good protection from sea spray and the wind. A heavier rain jacket is useful if you don't want to get your seat or head wet. Heavier rain gear is needed to keep warm as you get further from the Equator.

Rigging knife

Safety harness

Sailing gloves
Make sure your gloves allow for stretch and ease of movement.

Shoes
Reef runners work well in temperate climates. It doesn't matter if they get wet, and they have great grip. They also provide protection from stubbing your toes. Leather deck shoes are good when the temperatures get cooler.

Strobe light
A personal strobe attached to the shoulder strap of your safety harness is a must for doing night watches. Remember to bring spare batteries.

Whistle
The non-corroding type, attached to your safety harness.

NAVIGATION

Charts

Log Book

Star chart
It's so fun to learn the stars, especially ones that you never see at home. And so many are visible so far away from land.

Davis Guides
Davis makes a number of Quick Reference Guides printed on 8-1/2" x 11" hard plastic sheets. "Sightings At Sea" was great to have in the cockpit to identify dolphins, birds and ships as they were spotted.

MISCELLANEOUS

Books

Book light

Flashlight

Notepad & Pen

Keep a small notepad in your pocket to jot down things you want to remember later. Get a waterproof one for rainy weather. Putting your pen on a rope around your neck (stuffed inside your clothes) keeps it close at hand.

Mesh dive "goodie" bag
Great for carrying daily toiletry needs. Allows contents to dry and easy to find what you are looking for.

Dive gear
Take a mask and snorkel in case you need to dive on the boat in an emergency but also in case you get the opportunity to go snorkeling or diving.

Luggage
Backpacks or soft bags are best so they can be easily stuffed into lockers when not in use.

Camera
Make sure yours is water-resistant.

Film
Remember to bring lots of spare film for camera and video. Store them in a Ziploc bag.

Batteries
Remember spares for your flashlight, book light, strobe light, camera, video camera, etc.

Laundry bag

Walkman

Seasickness Remedies

TIPS ON GOING TO THE BAHAMAS

CHARTS: "The Bahamas" Chart Kit has solid travel info and GPS waypoints. We also purchased "Explorer Charts: Exumas" with GPS waypoints. The reference guide will answer many questions and instruct you on how to be a floating ambassador. Talk to the people at the store. Many of them have made the trip and have helpful information to share.

One Sea Sister advises "If anyone is planning to cruise the Exumas, I would advise they get a copy of the *Exuma Guide and the Explorer Charts*. We were without them, only the *Bahama Chartbook* and *Yachtsman's Guide*, which are not as detailed. Even though we are shallow draft, we don't like to take too many chances with unfamiliar territory."

THE CROSSING: Again, talk to others who have made the crossing as to suggested points of departure. As far as time, watch for a weather window and remember that the ocean takes at least one day to calm down after a blow.

CUSTOMS & IMMIGRATION: Enter port with yellow quarantine and Bahamas courtesy ensign flying. One person is allowed to leave the vessel. Painless if you're polite and have paperwork intact.

PROVISIONING: Many islands have no stores as they are uninhabited. "People" islands have staples. Fort Lauderdale, Nassau, and George Town in the Exumas are big provisioning or replacements stops. Meats and seafood are available at fair prices, considering most of it arrived by boat. Eggs are usually not refrigerated, milk may be sold frozen. Canned vegetables and juices are out of sight, i.e. $1.18 for a can of corn. Diesel prices vary, and gas can be as high as $2.90 a gallon. Water—there are some cisterns, and you may draw from them for free.

MONEY MATTERS: You will receive Bahamian money in the ATM, but laundromats use U.S. quarters.

COMMUNICATIONS: Good luck!!! Cellular *can* work, but you MUST sign up, and signing up could cost more than $500. Get an ATT calling card. "Batelco" is BAhamian TELephone COmpany and they will receive and hold faxes for your arrival. BATELCO, Shirley Street, Nassau, Tel. # 809/ 321-2021, Fax: 809/393-1651. Open every day, 8 a.m. - 8 p.m.

If you have a cell phone, be sure to inquire about an unadvertised "Snowbird Rate" that allows you to suspend your service for several months. Why pay for service if you're not going to use your phone? Call you customer service for more details.

Most marinas are set up for cruiser communication. UPS and Fed EX give *fast* service. Any mailing you do must have Bahamas postage. Tell family and friends, "No gifts—only mail." One **WOMEN ABOARD** member paid $4.00 duty for her burgee. Another cruiser paid $1.00 for two candy bars her kids sent with mail.

SNORKLING: No jewelry, no suits with metallic thread, and remember, after 4 p.m. the fellows in grey suits (sharks) start shopping for dinner.

Please remember you have left the rules and the Constitution of the United States behind. You are now a guest in a foreign country. You will be warmly received, so enjoy these wonderful people and their beautiful islands. Respect them, read up on their past history, and participate in island activities.

Getting messages to cruising friends in George Town, Bahamas is a fax away! List the name of the boat at the beginning of your message and fax to 242-336-2645. This is Exuma Markets Ltd., phone 242-336– 2033. Their e-mail address is exumamarket@batelnet.bs

Airlines to George Town

From Fort Lauderdale:
Island Express   954-359-0380
Air Sunshine   800-435-8900
                 954-434-8900
Lynx Air   888-596-9247
                 954-491-7576

Charters from Florida
Air Charter One 800-JETFLITE
                561-750-6200
Dolphin Atlantic 800-353-8010
                 954-359-8010

Charters from Bahamas
Cherokee Air   242-367-2089
Cleare Air   242-377-0341
Congo Air   242-377-8329

From Miami
American Eagle 800-433-7300
               787-749-1747
Bahamasair   800-222-4262
               305-593-1910

Trans Caribbean Air
               888-239-2929
               954-434-5271

CRUISING AND PROVISIONING SOUTH OF THE BORDER

<u>PROVISIONING</u>

- Provisioning in Mazatlan, La Paz, and Puerto Vallarta is excellent. They all have nice, big supermarkets and Mazatlan even has a Sam's Club. You can also get many items in Cabo, but it is so much more expensive than any major provisioning is not recommended.

- You can get just about anything you need at the supermarkets, which are very modern. This includes many American foods, although you will pay a higher price for items that are bought only by Americans. The best rule of thumb is to eat like the locals as much as you can, keeping in mind that there will be certain things that you may want to spend a little extra to have. Our big indulgence is Chips Ahoy chocolate chip cookies.

- There are a few items which are very difficult to find, or extremely expensive when you do. These items include canned tomatoes, chocolate chips, brown sugar, Bisquick, whole coffee beans, and lemon juice. There is a huge variety of dried beans, but canned beans (including baked beans) are not so common.

- Fresh produce is abundance and excellent. It is advised that you soak it to kill the bacteria. You can use a bleach and water solution, or they sell products at the supermarket, such as Microdyn. Microdyn can also be used to purify water.

- We have bought good chicken and pork at the supermarket. Beef is not aged and is sometimes tough, so you gamble a little bit there. We have had some excellent rib-eye steaks. Lunch meat, hot dogs, and bacon are sold at all of the supermarkets.

- Finally, if you see something you want, BUY IT, because it may not be there the next time you go to the store (kind of like Costco).

SERVICES

- Each major cruising port will have a daily local cruisers' net on the VHF (so far, always Channel 22). Typical topics include who's new, services offered or needed, general announcements, and trades (we can't conduct business in Mexico, only "trade") which is a great way to get rid of stuff you don't want or need anymore. They will also ask who can carry mail either to another Mexican port or back to the U.S. or Canada to be mailed, so it's a good idea to bring plenty of postage stamps.

- When we crossed the Mexican border, I didn't think I would ever see another washing machine or dryer. Not true. Laundromats are plentiful, especially in the marinas, and it is usually only a couple of extra pesos (25 cents) to have it done for you. It is hard to find liquid laundry soap, but the powdered soap here is cheap and very good. And speaking of soap, powdered or gel form dishwashing soap is most common, although I have started seeing liquid at the supermarkets—again, for a price!

CREEPY CRAWLERS

- There are two types of cruising boats here: those that HAVE roaches and those that ARE GOING TO GET roaches. The odds of you getting roaches are probably inevitable here since they can come on the boat in a variety of ways: cardboard boxes, the labels of canned goods, and even on your dock lines. I bought roach motels, spray and boric acid. So far, I've only used the boric acid and have bay leaves all over the place (having read about that in *WOMEN ABOARD*)! So far, so good.

152

- Mosquitoes haven't been a problem yet, but we are still in the cities. I brought a lot of mosquito coils, but you can also buy them here.

COMMUNICATING

- Mexico's phone company, TelMex, has finally lost its monopoly and will begin to have competition in 1997. Hopefully, this will bring down the price and increase the quality of the service, which is pretty poor right now. If you have a calling card, be sure it allows international calls.

- One of the most cost-effective ways to communicate quickly is by fax. The marinas will accept faxes for you for a small fee. They can also send faxes for you, again for a fee. We have also found a few places where we can use the phone line to log onto CompuServe to send and receive e-mail.

- Single-sideband radio is a great way to stay in touch with other cruisers. We tune into the Southbound Net just about every night. We have also set up radio schedules with other cruisers and have communicated with boats in the South Pacific as far away as 3,000 miles.

- One word of advice: Stay legal. In other words, don't use a ham radio on SSB frequencies. One of our cruising friends here in Mexico recently received a not-so-nice letter from the FCC telling him that he would lose his boat's radio license if he continued to do this. They are out there!

FIXING THINGS

Yes, it's true. No matter how well prepared you THINK you are, things will go wrong. We have had to repair a salt water pump (engine), refrigeration, heads, and a windlass motor to name a few major items. Bring spares of any important partsIf you leave from the West coast, stop by Downwind Marine in San Diego and set up an account (i.e. give them your credit card number.) You can order from them via SSB or letter and they'll bill your card and get it down to you via boat.

Those of you living in warm weather are probably more aware of the deterioration that can be caused by the sun. If you plan to spend the summer here, give strong consideration to items like a dinghy cover, gas can covers, and most important, an awning. If you plan to do or have any canvas work done while in Mexico, bring your own material. If you shop around, you can definitely get Sunbrella cheaper in the U.S.

REACH OUT AND TOUCH SOMEONE —
KEEPING THE COMMUNICATION LINES OPEN
WHILE CRUISING

Cruising is a wonderful lifestyle, filled with unique experiences and unforgettable sights. But, like any lifestyle, it is not without its drawbacks. When Sea Sisters are asked if there is anything they don't like about cruising, some of their answers are identical—they miss being in frequent contact with the people they care about.

Staying in touch in the United States is easy—just picked up the phone. But once you left the U.S., it quickly became apparent that the phone isn't a practical way to stay in touch on a cruising budget. So, what to do? Reach out and touch someone—keep the communication lines open while cruising

SATELLITE COMMUNICATIONS

One Sea Sister and her husband installed an Inmarsat C before they left California in January 1996 and they never regretted it. While the price tag was not insignificant, the ability to receive and transmit text at any time has been well worth the money. As the technology improves, Inmarsats are getting smaller and less expensive.

Sat C is a text-only communications system that allows you to transmit e-mail, faxes, and telexes and also to receive telexes and e-mail. You can also do mobile-to-mobile (one Inmarsat to another Inmarsat) communications and receive a lot of other information, including weather updates. One very important feature is that you can send an emergency distress message with the Inmarsat by pressing just two buttons.

In addition to being able to send you an e-mail messages, people back home can also contact you by calling a toll-free number and dictating a message (there is a charge for the message that is billed to the sender.)

There is a cost for sending and receiving faxes, telexes and e-mail and it can vary with the service provider. It is not unusual to use three different providers as prices and options do vary.

Inmarsat's greatest appeal is that it allows two-way communication 24 hours a day, 365 days a year. Because it is a satellite communications system, the higher frequencies it uses are not easily affected by the atmospheric conditions that impact radio propagation.

Inmarsat may be used in a lot of different ways. You can fax your mail service so that your mail will be at our destination when you arrive. You can also use it to order equipment and replacement parts so that they will be in port when you get there. You may use it to stay in touch with other cruisers who have Inmarsat. It can give you great peace of mind to know that friends and family can contact you anytime, anywhere, if needed.

HF (HIGH FREQUENCY) RADIO

Most boats have either a ham or SSB (Single Sideband) radio and some actually have one of each.

HAM RADIO

A ham radio allows licensed amateurs to use designated frequencies for various forms of communication including voice, Morse code, and digital (e.g. packet or pactor). The type of license you have (Novice, Technician, General, Advanced or Extra) determines which frequencies can be used. The Novice and Technician licenses provide very limited voice privileges, so you really need to get a General license which requires that you pass a written test and a Morse code test at 13 words per minute. It is important to keep in mind that ham frequencies are for personal use only. No commercial traffic is allowed.

While we enjoy using the ham frequencies to check into different nets and talk with other hams, we also use them to send and receive e-mail. While not nearly as reliable as the Inmarsat C, the price is right—it's free!!

To be able to send and receive e-mail though the ham radio, you need an additional piece of equipment called a Terminal Node Controller or TNC. Like any other type of radio communication, the atmospheric conditions have an effect on sending and receiving e-mail. If someone has a stronger signal than yours, you can get "bumped" and have to start all over again. Also, as more boats use digital communications, the ability to use ham frequencies for e-mail is becoming more difficult. There are a limited number of frequencies available at any one time. Some frequencies have been tied up for as long as 45 minutes processing a long e-mail message. So while we occasionally use the ham for short messages, we would never use it for a critical message.

We also use the ham radio to make phone calls to people back home. Thanks to the many ham operators who have the proper equipment, there are several nets on which you can make a phone patch. The only cost is that of the collect phone call from the person doing the patch to the person you are calling. Since the calls are usually brief and people are so glad to hear from us, the cost has never been an issue. Once you leave North America you will usually be able to do a phone patch only when in international waters since most countries do not allow third party traffic. It's pretty neat to call your mom from the middle of the Pacific Ocean!

SINGLE SIDEBAND RADIO

A single sideband radio allows you to use frequencies which have been designated by the FCC for marine use. No special licensing is required, other than including it on your boat's FCC license.

If you have a ham license, an SSB radio can also be used to transmit on the ham frequencies. However, the reverse is not true. While many people alter their ham radios so that they can use them to transmit on the marine frequencies, keep in mind that this is illegal and if caught you might lose your boat's FCC license. One cruiser we know of actually had his ham radio, TNC, and computer confiscated when the technician discovered it had been altered.

Unlike the ham frequencies, the SSB marine frequencies can be used for commercial traffic. When we were in Mexico we used our SSB several times to order from Downwind Marine in San Diego.

SSB radio can also be used for e-mail using systems such as PinOak and Globe Wireless. Since I have not personally used these systems, I talked to some cruisers who have. Most were pretty happy with them, but did emphasize that propagation is a factor and affects when you are able to send and receive e-mail. I was also told that this technology is an evolving one and there have been a lot of improvements concerning this. The best advice is to stay on top of things, talk to a variety of people, read magazines, and make a point to talk to sales representatives at boat shows, rendezvous, etc.

The Age Old Argument: Why Get a Ham License If You Have an SSB?

A lot of people with SSB radio don't see any reason to get a ham license. But if you are Mexico-bound, you will see how active the ham nets are, and realize there are many benefits in having a ham license. Fortunately in Mexico, the reciprocal license for U.S. hams gives you very broad privileges and even with my Novice license, one could operate as if she had a General license. Keep in mind that in other countries, the reciprocal licenses might not be as generous, so you might want to consider getting your General before leaving Mexico.

One Sea Sister really wished she had done it before she left the U.S. since there are more opportunities to take tests in the U.S. Also, once you get into cruiser mode, it's REALLY hard to do anything that resembles work and believe me, studying for your General license is definitely work! So get your General license before you go, even if you don't think you'll use it—you just never know.

THE WRITTEN WORD

FAXES

Faxes are still a very popular form of communication and available everywhere. They are usually much more economical than a phone call and are used for both personal and business communications. Most marinas have fax machines and there are many mail services and other businesses that offer faxing services.

E-MAIL

The good news is that this is a global situation and there are more and more services that allow you to send and receive e-mail. Most libraries will allow you to access your e-mail either free or for a nominal fee.

If you plan on being a marina for any length of time, consider getting a phone line. It will save you a lot of money on phone calls and faxes and allow you to stay in regular communication with our friends and family.

LETTERS

Finally, never underestimate the power of the pen! While it may not be the fastest form of communication, nothing warms the heart like a letter from home. Unlike a radio or computer communication, a letter can be read, shared with others, and saved to be read again.

Most people have their mail sent to a central location, then forwarded to them when they arrive in port. Many people have a friend or relative handle this, or you may choose to go with a mail service.

You will find there are different courier services in different parts of the world. A good mail service will know who to work with in terms of best cost and service.

Be sure to take plenty of U.S. stamps with you as people traveling back to the U.S. will usually carry mail back.

As you can see, there are a lot of ways to communicate while cruising. Some cruisers say that the reason they went cruising was to be away from phones, radios and computers and have chosen to keep their communications as simple as possible. Others like having lots of ways to stay in touch. We all have different priorities and fortunately there are lots of options available to fit our different needs and cruising budgets.

MORE CRUISING TIPS FROM WOMEN ABOARD

- The U.S. Dept. of State publishes "Tips for Travelers" pamphlets that cover a number of areas in the world. The pamphlets cost $1 each. Write: Superintendent of Documents, U.S. Govt. Printing Office, Washington, DC 20402 for a list of available pamphlets.

- Carry a road map and guide books covering the areas you cruise. You'll be able to determine where you are in relation to your chart.

- Keep a road atlas on board as well. NOAA reports often refer to counties. With a land map, you can track weather more accurately.

- Speaking of maps, give your family-back-home a map of the area you'll be cruising. Mount it on cork board and give it to them, along with a box of push-pins. When you call, write, or send photographs, they can pop in a pin to make a connection to the places your letter describes, relating them to the location of your last correspondence.

- To see as much as you can on a limited budget, eat out (but do it at breakfast or lunch) or buy a local book and local food to experiment with regional tastes.

- Weekends are an excellent time to scout out church picnics or fund-raisers in the areas in which you are traveling. These give you a prime opportunity to try a variety of local or ethnic food. You can also talk to people and learn what *they* like about their country, where *they* go for fun.

- Wooden clothes pins in the cockpit not only pin wet towels to the lifelines, they make a handy clip to close bags of snacks and also keep chart kit and guidebook pages in place.

- Alternating breakable and non-breakable items omits the need for space-consuming packing material. The plastic mustard bottle squeezes between a glass vinegar bottle and a jar of coffee, the pickles are wedged between tins of cookies, and the mayonnaise is buried in a bag of extra t-shirts.

- Velcro secures my computer and printer to the chart table so we can use them for weather fax while under way. For each, I wrapped the end of one Velcro fuzzy and one Velcro sticky piece around small wooden blocks. These blocks are screwed to the table surface and the Velcro pieces fasten together over the item to be secured.

- Luggage straps secure under-settee locker lids for passage-making. These lockers contain some of the heaviest items in the boat and would create havoc should the boat roll and the lid fly off. The straps, available at Wal-Mart, are made of webbing and plastic snap buckles. Each locker needs two straps. Put the ends around a block of wood, screwed the wood to the inside edge of the locker, and passed the straps up and around the lid to snap them together.

- This past summer, we supplied the blank tapes and a friend recorded movies for us from his satellite television. We'll enjoy them, as will new friends, in remote anchorages along the way.

- Friends were also great about bringing used paperback books. We have a good supply to read, as well as trade with other cruisers.

- Pretzel sticks take up less room than an equal weight of the curly kind.

- A supply of favorite candy bars or a good quality box of chocolate will seldom make it back off the boat.

- Boaters are ingenious in getting their favorite foods when away. Some have friends sending bags of favorite coffee blends, candies, and other goodies to their next destination. One respondent from Trinidad took care of someone's parrot while they flew home for awhile. What she wanted in payment was a box of Bisquick®.

- One of the most important isles in the store is paper products. Too much paper towels or toilet paper is a misnomer. And their price goes up in foreign ports or most any marina.

- Pringles offer a compact way to carry potato chips.

- Canned juice *concentrates* mix with 3 parts water, just like the frozen kind. These, however, don't require refrigeration until opened. Both Mott's and Welch's are good.

- Yogurt is easy to make along the way with powdered milk. You'll need a bit of non-pasteurized fresh yogurt or Rennet tablets (from the health food store) to get started. In warm climates, a yogurt maker is unnecessary. You only need a piece of tightly woven cotton cloth for draining the yogurt. A Sea Sister writes: "Last time we cruised, my beautiful Liz Claiborne scarf served quite well. (What else was I going to use it for?!) This time, I sewed a couple of bags from unbleached muslin, complete with drawstring, to hang over the sink."

- Cruiser's info relay: Ask friends to use postcards (rather than letters) when relaying important messages to the family member with whom you're most frequently in phone contact. The size of the postcard forces the writer to be concise, making the relay more likely to be accurate, and making the job easier for the person relaying the message to you over the phone.

- I started out with a pocketful of prepaid calling cards. Along the way a fellow boater told me about VoiceNet. The company charges 17.5 cents per minute (less than the prepaid cards I had) and bills in six-second increments. You can be billed or have the monthly charges put on your credit card. I have used VoiceNet since last November and am very pleased with their service. I also saw their ad in a recent Delta Airlines SKY magazine. They can be reached at 1-800-500-9028 or 1-800-530-8642.

- For the cruising liveaboard, one of the e-mail services like Yahoo and Hotmail is a perfect way to communicate. These services are free and are portable. We have had no difficulty in Caribbean finding business that rent, inexpensively, time on computer. Therefore, wherever we go, I can send and receive e-mail. Also, it gives me easy access to the Internet.

- "We finally found the solution to the problem of sending and receiving e-mail conveniently while cruising. The answer for us is the Sharp TM-20 Mobile Mail e-mail computer. It's a very small, compact unit only 6" long, 3" wide and ¾" thick and sends or receives e-mail anywhere in the  world. It also works on any phone except a digital cellular phone. All you have to do is prepare the messages, then take it to a phone where you open a small microphone on the back of the unit and adjust the movable receiver so that it's as close as possible to the phone's mouthpiece. It's then as simple as dialing an 800 number in the US or another 408 area code number outside the US, holding the phone to the back of the unit, and pressing a button on the front. A few seconds later, depending on how much you're sending and receiving, you hear a beep that tells you transmission is complete and ready to read or reply to. **Purchasing information:** Now you can have Pocket Mail AND a year of service for only $160! That's a savings of more than $100! Call Vicki at 1-888-213-5919 (9:00 – 5:00, PST) and be sure to give *WOMEN ABOARD*'s special promotional number: IWB 9690-716267.

- For those of you with wooden handrails: We've used beer coseys with the bottom removed, split lengthwise, to protect the wood from rope marks. It opens easily and clips itself over the handrail, then we secure the line from the fender to the handrail, tying it over the cosey. For long term use the cosey must be lined with some type of fabric, or the cosey material will stick to some finishes.

- When using a chart, track your progress with a pointer made from "Post-It Tape Flags." They are transparent, and have more "stickum" than regular Post-its.

- For really heavy-duty fenders for delivery trips, hurricane preparation and the like, we've been very happy with auto tires. These won't replace conventional fenders in normal usage, but they can be used as fantastic supplements. Tires are nearly indestructible, they protect a large area, they don't roll away from the area they're supposed to protect, and when you're through with them they can be disposed of (if you think you can live without them). Search out the smallest ones you can find in the junk pile at a tire dealer. Drill (and it isn't easy) a couple of drain holes equally spaced around the tread. Tie one end of maybe 1/2 inch small stuff through the center of the tire to support its weight when it's secured wherever you'll need it. Then, to protect your boat from the nasty black tire marks, make a plain drawstring bag of inexpensive (*cheap*) canvas to cover the tire (in a pinch, you can even wrap the tire, through the middle, with lengths of scrap fabric). We have occasionally had to use one of these tire fenders, *tied to hang outside of and on top of our regular fenders,* to protect us from some of the really rough docks (for instance, Morgan City when the Atchafalaya River was in flood). Worked great! Once, at a really rough spot, we used our fenderboard outside the tires to give our hull that few inches of extra protection it needed from a very intrusive bolt head.

- Make an effort to trade-off boat chores. If you can drive the boat while he readies the anchor, then you can learn to drive while underway. And you can learn to dock the boat. Practice on windless days with a minimum of audience!! Both of you can plan ahead for each day's run, or trade off parts of this job. And the same goes for "housework" chores. If mealtime comes along during your "on watch" period, why can't he make a sandwich and pour drinks? You need to be able to handle the boat for safety reasons, and he needs to give a hand doing dishes to give you a break once in a while. Of course, every couple gets used to dividing up the chores in their usual way, but give some serious thought to stretching your comfort zone and learn a new skill. Some day your safety and that of the boat may depend on it!

162

These tips were shared by a Sea Sister who is now in Trinidad:

- Keep 2 separate provisioning lists, one for galley items and one for items such as paper towels, shampoo, Ziploc® bags, insect repellent, etc.

- When shopping, dig to the back of the stack to compare the expiration dates, choosing the farthest date away.

- Photocopy all important documents, passports, credit cards, etc. Keep one copy in a safe place on board, and give a copy to a trusted person back home. The reasons will become very clear if any of these items are lost or stolen.

- Don't leave home without:

⇒ Parmalat or Nido milk

⇒ Ocean Spray and Welches juice concentrates

⇒ Lots of Cup of Soup

⇒ Canned chicken and beef. You can usually get fresh but keep some on board for a quick meal.

⇒ Sun-dried tomatoes and freeze dried mushrooms

⇒ Supply of self-stick postage stamps and peel-and-stick envelopes. Anything else will adhere together within weeks if you don't put wax paper between them.

⇒ Lots of non-greasy insect repellant (Cutter's brand gel)

⇒ Several collapsible 5-gallon jugs to cart water when a dock is not available.

⇒ Small roll of bubble wrap cut into rectangles. Wrap around glass jars and secure in place with tape or rubber bands to keep clinking to a minimum.

⇒ Ziploc® bags in the 2-gallon size. They are hard to find but *priceless* on board. I keep Kleenex, toilet paper and other things that could get damaged by moisture in nooks and crannies on the boat. If a leak occurs, your supply won't be damaged. They can also be used to transfer larger items to shore or other boats.

- K-mart has an amazing selection of canned goods that are suitable for provisioning. Try their canned bacon. If you can't find it on the shelf, try writing CELEBRITY FOODS, Elizabeth, NJ 07206. It has a long shelf-life and is good for a variety of things.

- Veg-Al is great for general cooking needs, as is rice.

- Take the lightest weight towels (the cheap kind you find in discount stores) because they absorb great and dry FAST.

- I'm sure you know that JOY dishwashing detergent lathers in salt water. Dries your skin, though, so take lots of good lotion. Speaking of lotion, take your favorite "small goods" (soap, lotions, etc. to pamper yourself!)

- Choose the liquid laundry detergent. Packs tight and secure and is easy to carry. Of course, bring a gallon or two of bleach for general boat use.

- We use Post-It Notes for bookmarks in our cruising guides while underway. Post-It Notes do not blow away in the wind.

- Charlie likes to put a rubberband around our cruising guide while it is in the cockpit and open to whichever page we are using. The rubberband keeps our place, and the guide doesn't seem to slide around as much either.

- Don't take "plastic" dinnerware. Indulge (or go Corelle). Creature comforts are a MUST. You don't want to feel like you're camping out. On that note, if you're a coffee or a tea drinker, take along a nice pot and brew your own. No instant, except for emergencies. Also, take a good thermos.

- Take lots of those packets of dried powdered gravy mixes, especially Hollandaise or Alfredo for all those LOBSTERS you're going to catch!

- American Cheese does not need to be refrigerated and has a long shelf-life. Take a bunch of it.

- Those "boxes" of wine are great, and when empty, you can put used motor oil in the bags for transport to a disposal facility.

- Watermaker

- Spices

- Laptop computer

- Good books to trade

- SSB radio. Even if you don't have a radio license, you can still listen to "Herb" for vital weather information. I'm sure you know who I'm talking about. Without Herb's wealth of information, our trip would have been a disaster!

- Take a hammock to tie to the mast and jib halyard. You'll be the envy of the harbor! I don't know why more people don't do this. It's a marvelous way to spend a sunny afternoon with a good book!

- Also at K-Mart you can pick up one of those little "carts" with wheels for about $20. These are great for transporting laundry, groceries, or even jerry cans. You can find them in the sporting/luggage department.

- Take lots of trash bags. They come in handy for more than just trash.

- Invest, if you haven't already, in a GOOD pair of UV sunglasses.

- If you rinse your fruits and veggies in a mild bleach solution and store them where they get air, they will last and last.

- Don't forget disposable rubber gloves.

- One of my favorite and simple meals (good for you, too) is canned black beans served over saffron rice with Hunt's Choice Cut Diced Tomatoes served over the beans topped with diced onion. It's really good, quick, and easy.

- Another is boxed Velveeta macaroni and cheese with a can of tuna and a can of Veg-Al mixed in. Of course, these are menus for times when you are unable to get "fresh" foods, but my, oh my, how good they taste on cold, rainy days!

- Take lots of packaged instant soups. They're great for a hot pick-me-up during a crossing or in rainy weather.

- Any way possible, take lots of "crispy" stuff. Be sure to pack it securely so they won't get stale, and you'll appreciate it in the long run. Goodies like chips and crackers are expensive in the islands, and since they've been shipped over anyway, are usually stale to begin with. However, take advantage of the "English" breakfast cookies, crackers and the like. They are "gourmet" and very inexpensive. Same holds true with canned Danish butter. It's great!

- Invest in a GOOD stainless steel can opener. The cheaper kinds quickly rust and are good for naught!

- I was able to find those packets of mayo at a wholesale facility.

- Taboule is great for pot-lucks. No cooking! Be prepared for lots of pot-lucks. Take some fancy items to "throw together" (i.e., a few cans of baby corn, black olives, olives, hearts of palm, you know, to enhance any meal and make it "special.")

- Squirt cheese

- Lots and lots of good music. Take your instrument if you play one.

- Don't forget a good wide-tipped magic marker. You'll need one for marking your propane tank, labeling and dating before storage, marking jerry cans or drop-off laundry bags, etc.

- As for clothes, pack lightly! I usually take a week's supply, along with one or two "nice" dresses and shoes for going out on the town. Also those plastic hangers don't rust and ruin your favorite outfits!

- Go to your doctor and request "Cipro." It's a wonderful, general-use antibiotic. Good for stomach upsets (the worst kind), bladder infections, etc. which are common when drinking "strange" water. Kinda expensive, but well worth it!

166

- Hopefully you're not a smoker, but if you are, take your own. Cigarettes are something like $4 and $5 a pack over there! If you are a smoker, maybe it's a GOOD TIME TO QUIT!

- Those "Baby Wipes" come in great for quick "personal" tidy-ups, and have good skin conditioners on them.

- For cleaning, X-14 is marvelous! But watch out, it bleaches as well as disinfects.

- Take a few of those long butane striker/lighters.

- Lay out an oriental rug and put a pretty bath mat in the head. Take some festive napkins and pretty placemats. Creature comforts are a blessing.

- Bleach ratio for storing fruits: 1 Tbsp. per 2 gallons of water. Best keepers are onions, potatoes (especially sweet potatoes—they will keep for <u>months</u>), turnips, carrots, celery, cabbage, cauliflower, beets, radishes, and tomatoes. Fruits: apples, citrus, and pears. Purchase apples, pears, tomatoes and peaches rock hard and unripe. Bananas should be purchased green, hard and on the stalk. Soak each 30 minutes in the bleach solution, pat dry and let stand 1 hour in the sun. Store them, if possible, in a cool, dark, ventilated place. Wrapping apples, citrus, green tomatoes and pears in newspaper helps, too. Try to stagger the ripening. Soaking bananas in salt water hastens ripening.

- Bleach will purify drinking water too: The ratio is:
  - 8 drops: 1 gallon
  - 1 2/3 tsp: 10 gallons
  - 4 tsp: 30 gallons
  - 2 Tsp: 50 gallons
  - 4 Tsp: 100 gallons

- Bill paying: Many cruisers choose to pay for fuel and other items with plastic. All companies have an 800 number that you can check for your balance. One cruising Sea Sister suggested enclosing a photocopy of the top portion of a previous statement with the check to make certain that the account is properly credited.

- An extra anchor

- Spare mooring lines, in sizes long enough for locks and unusual dockings, are important. Extra fenders, too.

- Marine sells a "Little John®" and "Lady J®," $3.99/each urinals for when the head is full, broken, or for those long nights on watch.

- Don't take fluffy towels. The older and cheaper, the better. They take up less space, and dry in no time.

- His and her binoculars, to keep you from constantly having to adjust the lens, are a wonderful luxury.

- Folding bicycles are great accessories. You can see the sites and exercise at the same time. Add a basket and you will have a place to carry your purchased supplies on your way home.

- For mailings, take tons of peel-and-stick stamps and no-lick envelopes.

- Velcro® secures things a bit firmer than the non-skid mats. For example, use in holding computers/printers to the chart table.

- Head lamps facilitate chart reading or entering the log on that long night watch.

- Take a battery-operated light to attach to your book.

- Extra pillows for propping up to read.

- Bungee cords. All sizes.

- Mosquito netting.

- Lip balms with SPF are not only handy as intended, but they coat zippers on dodgers and enclosures that get exposed to the sun.

- Lawn chairs that can be set up on the dock carry their weight when it comes time to tip one with your new neighbors.

- Red and green nail polish are great markers. All battery switches in one Sea Sister's boat are painted. It helps them, and their guests, to remember which is 12VDC or 110VAC. Use it to mark electrical wires, or change a plain light bulb into a port or starboard light.

- Take five gallons of spare fresh water, especially when going away from easy-to-get water areas.

- Wire hangers are handy to have aboard. One Sea Sister's husband has repaired everything from a sheared shaft coupling to electronic gear.

- Panty hose pieces are good to wrap around liquor bottles. If they break, glass is contained. All that is left is to clean the red wine off the white carpet.

- Consider the time of year you'll be out, as far as special occasions. Need pumpkin for the pie, or cranberry sauce? Birthday candles? Wrapping supplies or birthday cards? Any family traditions to maintain?

- Quarters—keep a supply in an unlabeled prescription bottle.

- Bring half the provisions you think you need. When visiting an area— GO NATIVE. Eat where the locals eat, not just where the boaters gather. Eat at the commissary vans parked on the streets, attend and participate in if you could, at all church suppers, book fairs, picnic BBQs. Every village in the Bahamas has someone who makes wonderful bread—buy it!

- To kill a fish you caught in a bloodless manner, spray Vodka down its mouth or gills. It will quiet down in a minute.

- Think about what foreign currency you will need, and take enough for convenience if you arrive during non-banking hours. We frequently cruise in a foreign country, so have a checking account there to make good exchange-rate payments for necessities.

- Computers are becoming commonplace boat necessities. Remember a backup disc to slip into your pocket. Keep paper and an extra ink cartridge for your printer on board. Take the power cord.

- A micro cassette recorder is handy. When you charter, record all shakedown information. Also good for grocery or repair lists, if you hear of a great spot to visit, or information on snapshots.

- Don't forget the charger adapters for any of the above.

- Think about purchasing an SSB receiver. This allows you to receive NMN weather and record it. Include headphones and recorder with built in microphone. By using a transparent 8½" x 11" plastic sleeve with chart inside, you can draw in the fronts and high/lows. Use a dry erase marker.

- Several companies (including Radio Shack®) makes head sets that allow the captain and first mate to confer without shouting while anchoring or motoring through shallow waters.

- Keep a notebook of what you forgot on this trip, and you'll have it for the next one.

- Have a grocery inventory on your computer. Include preferred brands or sizes if someone else does shopping duty.

- One Sea Sister keeps a computer list of recommended equipment and clothing for visiting guests. It includes such forgettable things as soft bags (easier to store than cases), fishing license, flash light, and fanny pack.

- For books, consider Chapman Piloting; a Bible; dictionary; the best possible medical/first aid book you can find; field guides to fish, birds, insects, plants, or sky/weather; a marine catalog; and information on the areas you travel, including marinas, harbors, and towns (even if you've been there before).

- Important personal papers, with copies left to a trusted person on shore, will prove invaluable. Include passport and credit card copies. Don't forget medical information and records, insurance policies, subscription and membership information. Carry them in Ziplocs or cover with clear contact paper.

170

- Keep a hometown telephone book onboard, with addresses, phone, fax, and email information for anyone you may need to contact, such as family doctors, attorney, financial and tax advisors.

- Paperbacks are good trading stock, either to individuals or to marina book exchanges.

- Many cruisers now carry boat cards. They beat writing names and numbers on scrap paper, inevitably soon lost.

- Keep your ATM withdrawal slips until your bank statement catches up with you and you can compare them. One Sea Sister was unable to withdraw money twice because the ATM's weren't communicating, but when their statement arrived, they had been dunned $600! Plus the bank fee! And because that dropped their account below a specified amount, they incurred a service charge and didn't get any interest on the account. It took three months of telephone/mail tag to straighten out, *despite* being able to produce the two $0.00 withdrawal slips. So be careful at ATM's!

* * *

How about a DC Voltage Booster which boosts your house batteries' 12 VDC power up to 15, 18, or 20 VDC to run your laptop directly? Imagine being able to eliminate BOTH your DC to AC inverter and your laptop's AC to DC power supply, or "brick"! We found one that is inexpensive and very efficient.

While at Comanche Cove Marina in St. Augustine, FL one Sea Sister's husband came across a flyer, which described the booster. He then contacted Sam Ulbring, the inventor of the booster, and after speaking with Sam on the telephone they purchased one. We are extremely pleased with the results.

Benefits of the Power Booster:

- Produces 15 or 18 or 20 volts DC from your house batteries to run your laptop directly from your ships battery

- SMALL size (our booster measures about 4" x 3" x 2")

- High Efficiency (much more efficient than inverting 12 VDC to 120 VAC then converting the 120 VDC back down to 15 or so VDC)

- Very low RFI (unlike inverters) so you can use your laptop with your Ham or SSB radio without interference

- Inexpensive

- Available as a kit or finished product.

To order one, contact Sam via:

Email: n4uau@afn.org

Snail mail:
> Sam Ulbing, N4UAU
> 5200 NW 43rd Street
> Suite 102-177
> Gainesville, FL 32606

Phone: 352-375-3351

Sam's booster is available as a parts kit, soldered up version, or a completely wired, tested, and mounted inside a project box (it's worth it unless you get a kick out of winding triodes.) If ordered wired and tested or as the complete box, Sam will build it for the voltage you specify for your computer. We bought the completely wired and tested version and the cost was $57 (and that included postage). It only took a week from the time we ordered it to receive it. Sam asked me to pass along that the price for the kit is $23 and the soldered up version is $33.   He will be happy to ship to the Bahamas and the Caribbean for a few dollars more.

When ordering, have the voltage and amperage required by your computer. Sam sends the booster with exposed wires for you to solder the correct plug for your laptop. We found one at Radio Shack and had no problems soldering it on.

Ham operators on the Waterway Net 7268 can also reach Sam at 7:45 Eastern time every day. Happy computing!

* * *

"With only a quick backward glance, we departed James Creek Marina in Washington, DC and headed south in October,1993. Our planned 18-month-cruise from DC to San Diego is now in its fourth year and we've just arrived in Puerto Rico. Along the way, we have made some fascinating discoveries:

172

- The best part of cruising is the sense of community—we have met the most interesting, friendliest, brightest, most enthusiastic people everywhere we have cruised. The trust and kindness that is so often missing on land is alive and well among cruisers. We have been given condos to live in, cars to use, rides, advice, assistance, comfort, laughter and memories galore.

- Your land-based friends don't have a clue! They think it's all umbrella drinks and tropical paradises. And, trying to describe what it is like to grip for 54 hours in 8' seas or the satisfaction of dropping the hook after your safe arrival, usually results in a glazed look, a slight shake of the head, and an occasional, "You really ARE crazy."

- Our boat is a totally self-sufficient world which needs love, care, and attention. The more we give her up front, the better she performs at sea. Lots of preventive maintenance can significantly reduce the chances of major problems. We try to put as many points as possible in the black box. Being married to a mechanical engineer helps a lot!

- You and your mate must be a team. If you both understand the boat's systems and know how to do just about everything, it will be fun and satisfying for both of you.

- ALWAYS respect the weather! Mother nature rules!

- There is nothing wrong with staying another day at anchor to avoid a tough passage.

- Have good charts and cruising guides. You will be amazed at how this information will enhance your cruise and relieve your anxiety about a tight anchorage or a strange port.

- Try not to have a schedule that will make you go when or where you shouldn't. Guests must be flexible. Invite family and friends who will enjoy cruising and who know enough about boats to be helpful, not hazardous. You will all have more fun.

- It will cost you more than you think up front, so be prepared for sticker shock. Know your financial comfort zone and stick to it. We stopped in St. Petersburg for two years to do some consulting and refill the cruising kitty. Cruising is no fun if you worry about the cost of every dinner out or part you have to order.

- One you leave the Land of Stuff, you really won't miss much. There are too many new things to fill your time. Mostly, I miss...I honestly can't think of anything!

- When you do go ashore, take advantage of what the local area has to offer. Rent a car or take a tour. Try the local cuisine. Ask lots of questions of other cruisers and local residents. We have learned so much about the places we have anchored from the people there.

- Keep a journal. You will love reading it a year from now.

- It is okay to do nothing...when you finally get the chance. Cruising can be hard work, so when you have a calm, safe anchorage, take a nap, read a book, play a game, write a friend, look at the stars, hug your mate, enjoy life.

Above all, relish this opportunity. It is truly a magic time. Wouldn't it be nice if everyone could experience the people, challenges, and rewards that we do? I think our world would be a better one.

Index

SUSAN GARRIQUES has been drawing since she was a teenager and is primarily a self-taught artist. Most of her work has been with graphite (pencil), although in the past several years, she has been experimenting with watercolor, pen and ink, and acrylics. This book is the second book she has illustrated. Susan had the honor of having her design chosen for the Easter Seals Society of the Florida Keys annual Christmas ornament in 1999. That same year she participated in the Clean Florida Keys dumpster painting project. Although she would truly love to devote all her time to art, the cruising kitty demands to be fed. Susan is working as a web site designer until the kitty gets full enough to go cruising again.

MARIA RUSSELL is a former special-education teacher from St. Louis, Missouri. Her husband introduced her to sailing in the late 1970's and she has been hooked on boating ever since. Along with her husband, their two children, and a menagerie of pets (a dog, a cat, lizards, gerbils, and even an ant farm), she lived and cruised aboard a trawler for nearly ten years. Curious to know if other women loved boating as much as she did, Maria founded *WOMEN ABOARD*® in 1994 and has been amazed by its tremendous growth and far-reaching impact on boating women all over the world. She lives in North Palm Beach, Florida.